■ SCHOLASTIC

The Jumbo Book of Sight Word Practice Pages

200 Top High-Frequency Words With Quick Assessments

Immacula A. Rhodes

New York • Toronto • London • Auckland • Sydney
Mexico City • New Delhi • Hong Kong • Buenos Aires

In memory of Keith—
wonderful father, loyal friend

*His master said to him, "Well done,
good and faithful servant."*
—Matthew 25:21

Cover design by Niloufar Safavieh
Interior design by Holly Grundon
Interior illustrations by Teresa Anderko, Maxie Chambliss, Kate Flanagan, Rusty Fletcher,
James Graham Hale, Lucia Kemp Henry, Anne Kennedy, and Karen Sevaly

ISBN 978-0-545-48972-0

5 6 7 8 9 10   40   21 20 19 18 17 16

contents

Sight Word Practice Pages

SIGHT WORD	PAGE	SIGHT WORD	PAGE

Introduction

About Sight Words

The Jumbo Book of Sight Word Practice Pages is a collection of engaging activities designed to help kids master the top 200 high-frequency words found on the Dolch Basic Sight Word Vocabulary List. A variety of activities, such as color-coded pictures, word mazes, connect-the-dot puzzles, word matches, and fill-in-the-blank sentences, offers children a fun, motivating way to get the repeated practice they need to build their sight word vocabulary.

Sight words, or high-frequency words, are the words most commonly encountered in any text. Children often have difficulty decoding many of these words since they do not follow regular rules of spelling. In his book *Phonics From A to Z* (Scholastic, 2006, revised), reading specialist Wiley Blevins notes that the benefits of having a bank of sight words at the ready are significant for children who are learning to read. Accurate and automatic recognition of sight words that are encountered in context enables a child to read more smoothly and at a faster rate, helping the child remember more of what he or she has just read and make sense of it. This is vital for young children to become fluent readers and comprehend the text they read.

The activities in this resource give children lots of opportunities to recognize, write, and spell sight words, as well as read the words in context. The words—taken from the Dolch Basic Sight Word Vocabulary List—are presented in the order of their frequency (see page 10 for a list of words by grade level), but you can introduce the pages in any order that best suits children's needs. Sight word cards, assessment charts, and recording forms are also included to help you reinforce learning and keep track of children's progress.

Many sight words are difficult for children to decode since they don't follow regular rules of spelling. Most are known as "function words" rather than "content words." And though they may not appear to carry a clear meaning, these words have a strong impact on the flow and coherence of the texts children read. The words on the Dolch Basic Sight Word Vocabulary List account for more than 50% of the words found in textbooks today.

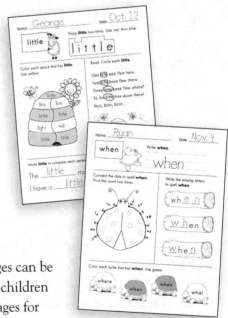

Each reproducible, two-sided page features a specific sight word. The pages can be used with the whole class, in small groups, or in a learning center where children complete them individually or in pairs. Or, children can complete the pages for homework. The activities are ideal for children of all learning styles, for ELL students, and for RTI instruction. And best of all, they connect to the Common Core State Standards for Reading (Foundational Skills) to help you meet the recommended learning goals for your students.

What's Inside

Each two-sided page in this resource features a specific sight word and activities that give children repeated practice in reading, writing, and spelling that word. To use, simply choose the word you want to teach, locate those pages in the book (see Contents, pages 3–6), and make double-sided copies. The only materials children need to complete the activities are crayons or colored pencils. Following are the types of activities included on the pages, with the skills they reinforce listed in parentheses:

Word Tracing (*word configuration, letter formation, spelling, word recognition*): Children are introduced to the target word and its shape at the top of the first page for each word. To complete this activity, children trace the word two times: first in red, then in blue.

Color-by-Word and Color-Coded Pictures (*word recognition, visual discrimination*): Children color items or spaces in a picture that are labeled with the target word. If desired, they can then color the remaining art with the colors of their choice. For the color-coded pictures, a color pattern may appear in some while a hidden object or animal appears in others.

Word Paths (*word recognition, fine motor*): In one form of this activity, children find the target word on an item and trace the path from that item to a specific location, such as from a leaf to a basket. In a second form, they draw a line path from an animal to the object labeled with the word (for instance, from a duck to a puddle).

Word Mazes (*word recognition*): To complete the mazes, children find the path that leads from a starting point to an end point by coloring the spaces or tracing the lines that are labeled with the target word.

Circle the Word (*word recognition, comprehension, fluency*): In the middle right section of the first page, children read a passage or poem and circle the target word in the text each time it appears. Picture clues offer support to help them decode words.

Fill-in-the-Blank Sentences (*writing, spelling, comprehension, fluency*): At the bottom of the first page, children complete each sentence by writing the sight word on the blank line. Then they read the sentence, using the picture clue to help with the meaning of the sentence.

Write the Word (*writing, spelling*): Children write the word independently on the lines at the top of the second page. Note that two sets of lines are provided for children to write the one-and two-letter words twice.

Connect-the-Dots (*spelling, fine motor*): Two types of connect-the-dot activities are featured. In one type, children connect the dots, spelling the target word twice, to reveal a picture. In the other type, they start at an object—such as a raindrop or bowling ball—and connect the dots to spell the word, which then creates a path to an end point (such as the ground or a bowling pin).

Word Matches (*word recognition*): In these activities, children color pictures that have matching words (such as the target word on both lenses of a pair of glasses) or draw lines to match objects that have been labeled with the target word—such as balloons—to a specific location, such as strings that are attached to a fence labeled with that word.

Word Finds (*spelling, word recognition, visual discrimination*): Children search the word-find puzzle and circle the target word each of the five times it appears.

Spelling Paths

(spelling, word recognition): To complete these activities, children trace the path with the letters that spell the target word.

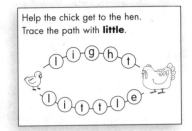

Write the Missing Letters *(spelling, letter formation)*: In these activities, found on the second page of the activity sheets, children write the missing letters to complete the spelling of the target word. For one- and two-letter words, they trace the first word, then write the word several more times by filling in the letters on the lines.

Spelling Match-Ups *(spelling, word recognition)*: Children color the sets or pairs of items that have the letters that spell the target word.

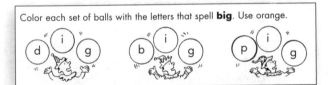

In addition to the activity pages, this resource also includes the following reproducible materials to help you teach the sight words and assess children's learning:

Sight Word Cards: Use the sight word cards (pages 11–20) for flash cards, in word matching games, or to post on your word wall. Each page of cards corresponds to the assessment charts on pages 21–30. You might color-code the cards by copying each set on a different color of paper or labeling them with sticky dots of a specific color.

Assessments: These easy-to-use charts (pages 21–30) feature twenty words per page. Use them to record baseline data, as well as to track children's progress as they build their sight word skills. If desired, use the corresponding sight word cards to administer each assessment. Also, you might color-code the charts to go along with the sight word card sets.

Record Sheets: Use the Sight Word Record Sheet (page 31) to evaluate children's ability to spell the sight words in each set. On copies of the Sight Word Sentence Record Sheet (page 32), have children write their own sentences (or sentences you dictate) using the target words.

Connections to the Common Core State Standards

The Common Core State Standards Initiative (CCSSI) has outlined learning expectations in English Language Arts for students at different grade levels. The activities in this book align with the following Foundational Skills for Reading for students in grades K–2. For more information, visit www.corestandards.org.

PHONICS AND WORD RECOGNITION

RF.K.3, RF.1.3, RF.2.3. Know and apply grade-level phonics and word analysis skills in decoding words.

RF.K.3c. Read common high-frequency words by sight (e.g., *the, of, to, you, she, my, is, are, do, does*).

RF.1.3g, RF.2.3f. Recognize and read grade-appropriate irregularly spelled words.

FLUENCY

RF.K.4. Read emergent-reader texts with purpose and understanding.

RF.1.4, RF.2.4. Read with sufficient accuracy and fluency to support comprehension.

RF.1.4a, RF.2.4a. Read grade-level text with purpose and understanding.

RF.1.4c, RF.2.4c. Use context to confirm or self-correct word recognition and understanding, rereading as necessary.

220 Dolch Words by Grade in Order of Frequency

Pre-Primer	Primer		First Grade	Second Grade		Third Grade
the	he	no	of	would	us	if
to	was	came	his	very	buy	long
and	that	ride	had	your	those	about
a	she	into	him	its	use	got
I	on	good	her	around	fast	six
you	they	want	some	don't	pull	never
it	but	too	as	right	both	seven
in	at	pretty	then	green	sit	eight
said	with	four	could	their	which	today
for	all	saw	when	call	read	myself
up	there	well	were	sleep	why	much
look	out	ran	them	five	found	keep
is	be	brown	ask	wash	because	try
go	have	eat	an	or	best	start
we	am	who	over	before	upon	ten
little	do	new	just	been	these	bring
down	did	must	from	off	sing	drink
can	what	black	any	cold	wish	only
see	so	white	how	tell	many	better
not	get	soon	know	work		hold
one	like	our	put	first		warm
my	this	ate	take	does		*full*
me	will	say	every	goes		*done*
big	yes	under	old	write		*light*
come	went	please	by	always		*pick*
blue	are		after	made		*hurt*
red	now		think	gave		*cut*
where			let			*kind*
jump			going			*fall*
away			walk			*carry*
here			again			*small*
help			may			*own*
make			stop			*show*
yellow			fly			*hot*
two			round			*far*
play			give			*draw*
run			once			*clean*
find			open			*grow*
three			has			*together*
funny			live			*shall*
			thank			*laugh*

Note: The italicized words are not featured in this book.

Word Cards: Sight Word Assessment Chart 1

little	up
down	look
can	is
see	go
not	we

you	the
it	to
in	and
said	a
for	I

Word Cards: Sight Word Assessment Chart 2

play	here
run	help
find	make
three	yellow
funny	two

blue	one
red	my
where	me
jump	big
away	come

do	there
did	out
what	be
so	have
get	am

they	he
but	was
at	that
with	she
all	on

Word Cards: Sight Word Assessment Chart 4

four	into
saw	good
well	want
ran	too
brown	pretty

are	like
now	this
no	will
came	yes
ride	went

Word Cards: Sight Word Assessment Chart 5

him	under
her	please
some	of
as	his
then	had

white	eat
soon	who
our	new
ate	must
say	black

Word Cards: Sight Word Assessment Chart 6

old	how
by	know
after	put
think	take
let	every

an	could
over	when
just	were
from	them
any	ask

Word Cards: Sight Word Assessment Chart 7

your	has
its	live
around	thank
don't	would
right	very

fly	going
round	walk
give	again
once	may
open	stop

Word Cards: Sight Word Assessment Chart 8

goes	cold
write	tell
always	work
made	first
gave	does

wash	green
or	their
before	call
been	sleep
off	five

Word Cards: Sight Word Assessment Chart 9

these	why
sing	found
wish	because
many	best
if	upon

pull	us
both	buy
sit	those
which	use
read	fast

Word Cards: Sight Word Assessment Chart 10

drink	keep
only	try
better	start
hold	ten
warm	bring

seven	long
eight	about
today	got
myself	six
much	never

Sight Word Assessment Chart 1

Student: _____   Teacher: _____   Grade: _____

Sight Word	Date	Date	Date
1. the			
2. to			
3. and			
4. a			
5. I			
6. you			
7. it			
8. in			
9. said			
10. for			
Score	____/10	____/10	____/10

Sight Word	Date	Date	Date
11. up			
12. look			
13. is			
14. go			
15. we			
16. little			
17. down			
18. can			
19. see			
20. not			
Score	____/10	____/10	____/10

Sight Word Assessment Chart 2

Student: _____   Teacher: _____   Grade: _____

Sight Word	Date	Date	Date
21. one			
22. my			
23. me			
24. big			
25. come			
26. blue			
27. red			
28. where			
29. jump			
30. away			
Score	____/10	____/10	____/10

Sight Word	Date	Date	Date
31. here			
32. help			
33. make			
34. yellow			
35. two			
36. play			
37. run			
38. find			
39. three			
40. funny			
Score	____/10	____/10	____/10

Sight Word Assessment Chart 3

Grade: _____   Teacher: _____

Sight Word	Date	Date	Date	Date
51. there				
52. out				
53. be				
54. have				
55. am				
56. do				
57. did				
58. what				
59. so				
60. get				
Score	___/10	___/10	___/10	___/10

Student: _____

Sight Word	Date	Date	Date
41. he			
42. was			
43. that			
44. she			
45. on			
46. they			
47. but			
48. at			
49. with			
50. all			
Score	___/10	___/10	___/10

Sight Word Assessment Chart 4

Student: _____ Grade: _____ Teacher: _____

Sight Word	Date	Date	Date
61. like			
62. this			
63. will			
64. yes			
65. went			
66. are			
67. now			
68. no			
69. came			
70. ride			
Score	___/10	___/10	___/10

Sight Word	Date	Date	Date
71. into			
72. good			
73. want			
74. too			
75. pretty			
76. four			
77. saw			
78. well			
79. ran			
80. brown			
Score	___/10	___/10	___/10

Sight Word Assessment Chart 5

Student: _____

Sight Word	Date ___ /10	Date ___ /10	Date ___ /10
81. eat			
82. who			
83. new			
84. must			
85. black			
86. white			
87. soon			
88. our			
89. ate			
90. say			
Score	___ /10	___ /10	___ /10

Grade: _____ Teacher: _____

Sight Word	Date ___ /10	Date ___ /10	Date ___ /10
91. under			
92. please			
93. of			
94. his			
95. had			
96. him			
97. her			
98. some			
99. as			
100. then			
Score	___ /10	___ /10	___ /10

Sight Word Assessment Chart 6

Student: _____ Grade: _____ Teacher: _____

Sight Word	Date	Date	Date
101. could			
102. when			
103. were			
104. them			
105. ask			
106. an			
107. over			
108. just			
109. from			
110. any			
Score	___/10	___/10	___/10

Sight Word	Date	Date	Date
111. how			
112. know			
113. put			
114. take			
115. every			
116. old			
117. by			
118. after			
119. think			
120. let			
Score	___/10	___/10	___/10

Sight Word Assessment Chart 7

Student: _____ Grade: _____ Teacher: _____

Sight Word	Date	Date	Date
121. going			
122. walk			
123. again			
124. may			
125. stop			
126. fly			
127. round			
128. give			
129. once			
130. open			
Score	___/10	___/10	___/10

Sight Word	Date	Date	Date
131. has			
132. live			
133. thank			
134. would			
135. very			
136. your			
137. its			
138. around			
139. don't			
140. right			
Score	___/10	___/10	___/10

Sight Word Assessment Chart 8

Grade: _____ Teacher: _____

Sight Word	Date	Date	Date	Date
151. cold				
152. tell				
153. work				
154. first				
155. does				
156. goes				
157. write				
158. always				
159. made				
160. gave				
Score	___/10	___/10	___/10	___/10

Student: _____

Sight Word	Date	Date	Date
141. green			
142. their			
143. call			
144. sleep			
145. five			
146. wash			
147. or			
148. before			
149. been			
150. off			
Score	___/10	___/10	___/10

Sight Word Assessment Chart 9

Student: _____   Grade: _____   Teacher: _____

Sight Word	Date	Date	Date
161. us			
162. buy			
163. those			
164. use			
165. fast			
166. pull			
167. both			
168. sit			
169. which			
170. read			
Score	___/10	___/10	___/10

Sight Word	Date	Date	Date
171. why			
172. found			
173. because			
174. best			
175. upon			
176. these			
177. sing			
178. wish			
179. many			
180. if			
Score	___/10	___/10	___/10

Sight Word Assessment Chart 10

Student: _____   Grade: _____   Teacher: _____

Sight Word	Date	Date	Date
181. long			
182. about			
183. got			
184. six			
185. never			
186. seven			
187. eight			
188. today			
189. myself			
190. much			
Score	___/10	___/10	___/10

Sight Word	Date	Date	Date
191. keep			
192. try			
193. start			
194. ten			
195. bring			
196. drink			
197. only			
198. better			
199. hold			
200. warm			
Score	___/10	___/10	___/10

Sight Word Record Sheet

Name: _____

Date: _____

Sight Words
1. _____
2. _____
3. _____
4. _____
5. _____
6. _____
7. _____
8. _____
9. _____
10. _____

Sight Word Record Sheet

Name: _____

Date: _____

Sight Words
1. _____
2. _____
3. _____
4. _____
5. _____
6. _____
7. _____
8. _____
9. _____
10. _____

Sight Word Sentence Record Sheet

Name: _____   Date: _____

Sight Word Sentences
1. _____
2. _____
3. _____
4. _____
5. _____
6. _____
7. _____
8. _____
9. _____
10. _____

Name: _____   Date: _____

 **the**

Trace **the** two times. Use red, then blue.

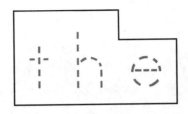

Color each bone that has **the**. Use yellow.

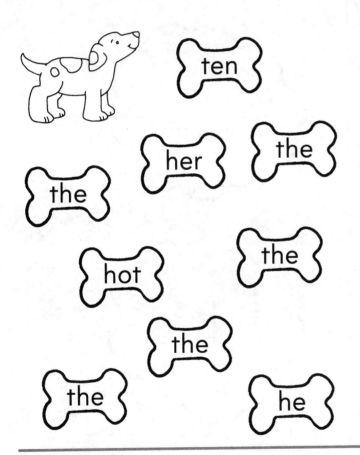

ten

her

the

the

hot

the

the

the

he

Read. Circle each **the**.

See the bone.

Get the bone.

Hide the bone.

Dig, dog, dig!

Write **the** to complete each sentence.

I see _____ ball.

Look at _____ cat.

Name: _____ Date: _____

the

Write **the**.

_____
- - - - - - - - - - - - - - - - -
_____

Find each leaf that has **the**. Trace the path from that leaf to the basket.

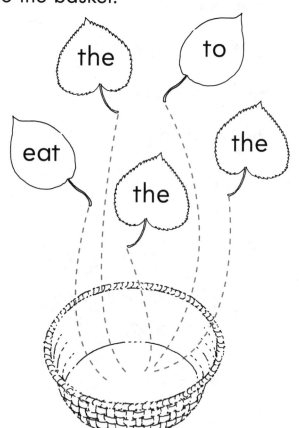
the to
eat
the
the

Write the missing letters to spell **the**.

t ___ ___

___ h ___

Color the two socks with the letters that spell **the**. Use red.

t

he

en

th

an

e

Name: _____   Date: _____

Trace **to** two times. Use red, then blue.

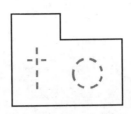

Color each butterfly wing that has **to**. Use purple.

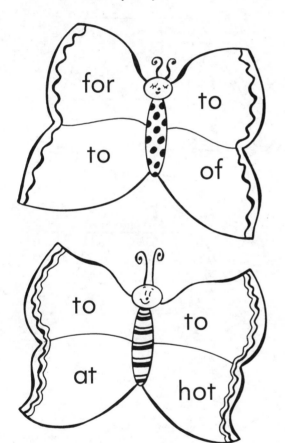

Read. Circle each **to**.

Down to the flowers.

Up to the tree.

Off to the sky.

Fly away. Whee!

Write **to** to complete each sentence.

The boy went _____ the store.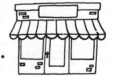

I like _____ ride the bus.

Name: _____ Date: _____

Write **to** two times.

_____

- - - - - - - - - - - - - - - - - - -

_____

Find each coin that has **to**. Trace the path from that coin to the bank.

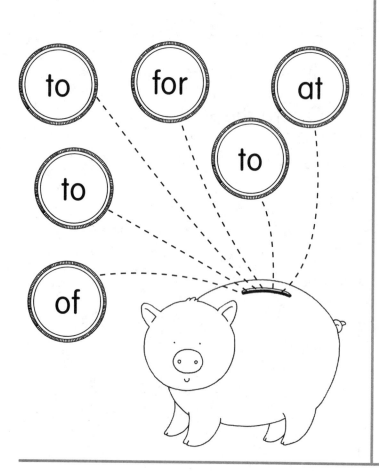

Write **to** on each tent.

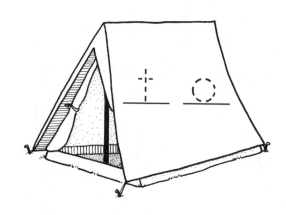

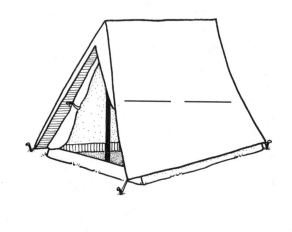

Color each pair of blocks with the letters that spell **to**. Use green.

Name: _____ Date: _____

 Trace **and** two times. Use red, then blue.

and

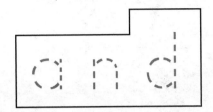

Color each gumball that has **and**.
Use red.

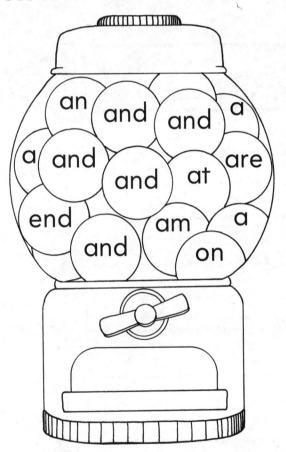

an and and a
a and are
and at
end am a
and on

Read. Circle each **and**.

Gum for you

and gum for me.

One for me

and one for you.

Ready, set, and chew!

Write **and** to complete each sentence.

I want some milk _____ cookies.

Is this your bat _____ ball?

Name: _____   Date: _____

and

Write **and**.

_____

- -

_____

Circle each **and**.
Find the word four times.

b	a	m	d
a	n	d	o
e	d	p	b
o	b	a	r
p	a	n	d
a	n	d	o
r	p	e	b

Write the missing letters
to spell **and**.

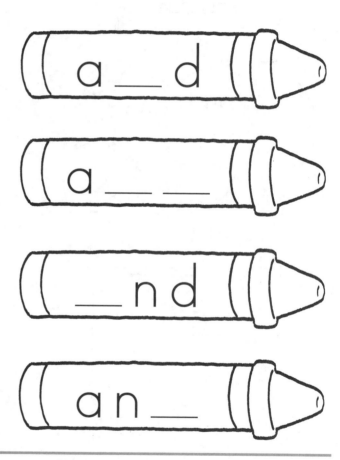

a __ d

a __ __ __

__ n d

a n __

Color each flower with the letters that spell **and**. Use yellow.

Name: _____ Date: _____

Trace **a** two times. Use red, then blue.

Color each space that has **a**.
Use green.

I	a	on
a	a	at	am
an	am	a	I
a	at	a

Read. Circle each **a**.

It has a head.

It has a tail.

It can hide

inside a shell.

What is it?

It is a turtle!

Write **a** to complete each sentence.

Can we play _____ game?

Dad gave me _____ drum.

Name: _____   Date: _____

Write **a** two times.

_____   _____

_ _ _ _ _ _ _ _ _   _ _ _ _ _ _ _ _ _

_____   _____

Help the crab get to the beach.
Color each space that has **a**.
Use brown.

Write **a** on each star.

Color each toy that has **a**. Use purple.

 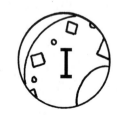  

I

Trace **I** two times. Use red, then blue.

Color each music note that has **I**.
Use purple.

Read. Circle each **I**.

I like to hum.

I like to sing, too.

I like to move

and dance with you.

Write **I** to complete each sentence.

_____ like to eat pizza.

This is the book _____ want.

Name: _____ Date: _____

 **I**

Write **I** two times.

_____   _____
- - - - - - - - -   - - - - - - - - -
_____   _____

Help the dog get to its house.
Trace the path that has **I**.

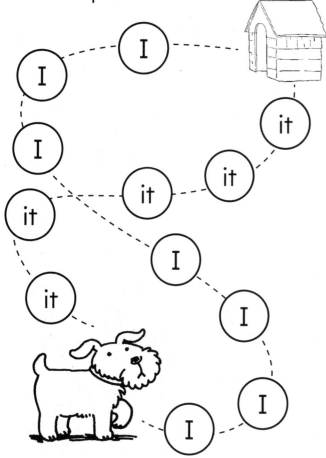

Write **I** on each heart.

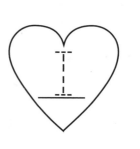 

Color each part of the caterpillar that has **I**. Use orange.

I   it   is   I   in   to   I   in   is   I

Name: _____   Date: _____

Trace **you** two times. Use red, then blue.

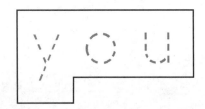

Color each bubble that has **you**.
Use blue.

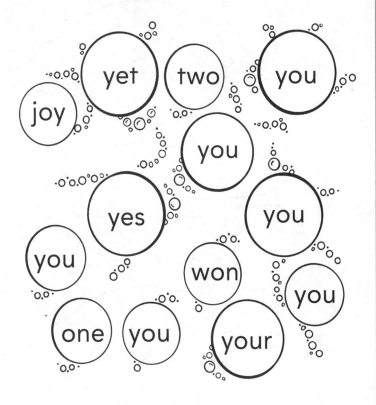

Read. Circle each **you**.

First, you blow one bubble.

Then you blow two.

All the bubbles that you blow

are just for you!

Write **you** to complete each sentence.

I have a drink for _____.

Did _____ see the horse?

Name: _____ Date: _____

you

Write **you**.

_____

_ _ _ _ _ _ _ _ _ _ _ _ _ _ _ _ _

_____

Connect the dots to spell **you**.
Find the word two times.

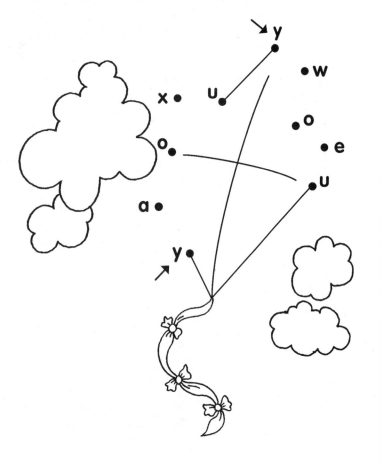

Write the missing letters
to spell **you**.

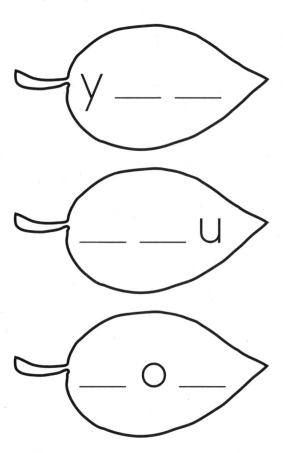

y ___ ___

___ ___ u

___ o ___

Color each acorn that has **you**. Use brown.

put

you

you

use

you

Name: _____ Date: _____

Trace **it** two times. Use red, then blue.

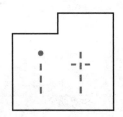

Color each space with **it**.
Use yellow.

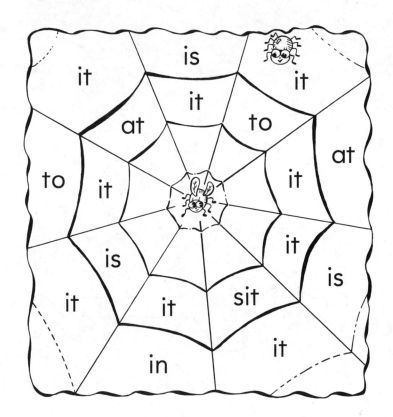

Read. Circle each **it**.

A spider makes it.

Then she sits on it.

In crawls a bug.

He can't get out of it.

It is a web!

Write **it** to complete each sentence.

What time is _____?

Here's a hat. Put _____ on.

Name: _____ Date: _____

Write **it** two times.

_____   _____

Draw a line from each duck to the puddle that has **it**.

 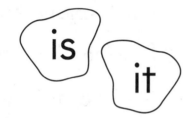

 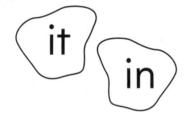

Write **it** on each duck.

Color each owl that has **it**. Use red.

it   sit   it   is   it   at   it   if

Name: _____ Date: _____

Trace **in** two times. Use red, then blue.

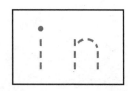

Color each egg that has **in**.
Use orange.

Read. Circle each **in**.

What was in the nest?

Eggs were in the nest.

What was in the eggs?

Chicks were in the eggs.

Now they are out!

Peep, peep, peep.

Write **in** to complete each sentence.

The dog is _____ his bed.

I have a book _____ my bag.

Name: _____   Date: _____

Write **in** two times.

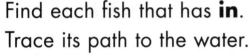

_____   _____

_____   _____

_____   _____

Find each fish that has **in**.
Trace its path to the water.

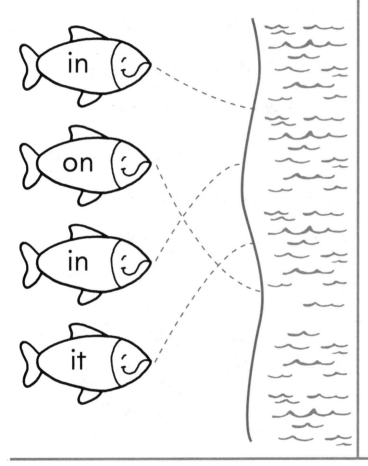

Write **in** on each yo-yo.

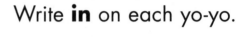

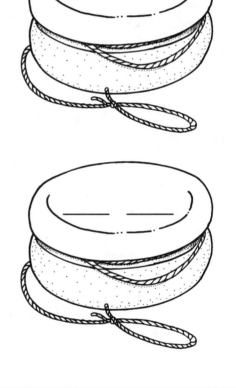

Color each train car that has **in**. Use purple.

| in | is | on | in | in |

Name: _____ Date: _____

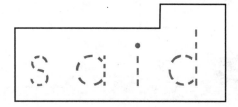
said

Trace **said** two times. Use red, then blue.

said

Help the cow get to the barn.
Color each space that has **said**.
Use green.

→said	sat	sad
said	said	saw	as
said	sad	day	sat
said	said	said	

Read. Circle each **said**.

The pig said, "Oink."

The cow said, "Moo."

The sheep said, "Baa."

And the rooster said,

"Cock-a-doodle-doo!"

Write **said** to complete each sentence.

Dad _____ we can have some pie.

I _____ I need a new coat.

Name: _____   Date: _____

said

Write **said**.

_____

_ _

_____

Color each kite that has **said**. Draw a string from that kite to the kangaroo.

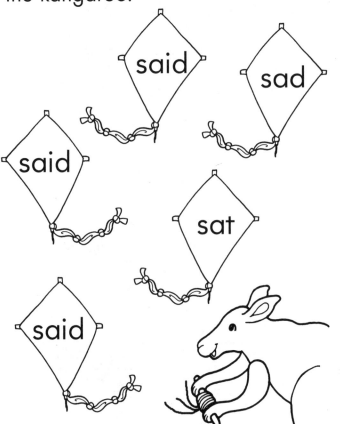

Write the missing letters to spell **said**.

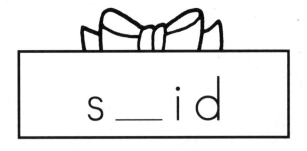

s __ i d

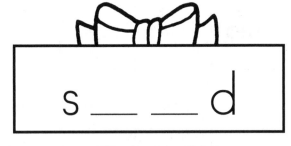

s __ __ __ d

__ a i __

Color each bear that has **said**. Use brown.

Name: _____ Date: _____

Trace **for** two times. Use red, then blue.

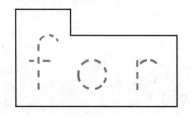

Color each star that has **for**.
Use yellow.

Read. Circle each **for**.

Go for a ride.

What do you see?

Look for the stars.

Get one for me.

Write **for** to complete each sentence.

This apple is _____ you.

Please get my coat _____ me.

Name: _____   Date: _____

Write **for**.

_____

- - - - - - - - - - - - - - - - - -

_____

Circle each **for**.
Find the word five times.

t f o r
n o h a
e r t m
f o r h
a t e f
f o n o
t f o r

Write the missing letters
to spell **for**.

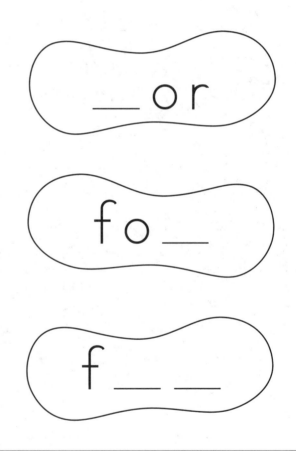

__ o r

f o __

f __ __ __

Help the car get to the Finish line. Trace the path that has **for**.

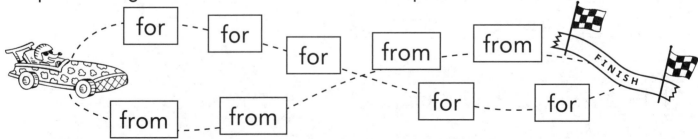

Name: _____   Date: _____

Trace **up** two times. Use red, then blue.

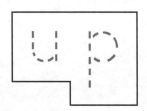

Color each leaf that has **up**.
Use green.

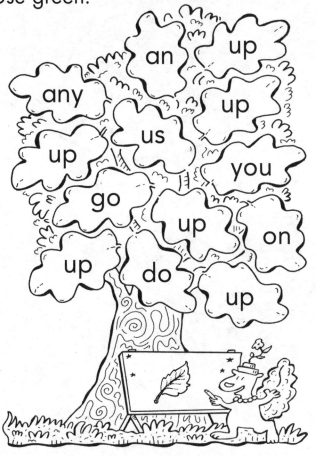

any · an · up · up · us · up · go · you · up · do · up · on

Read. Circle each **up**.

A bird goes up.

A bee goes up.

A butterfly goes up.

A leaf goes down.

Write **up** to complete each sentence.

The balloon went _____ high.

Look _____ at the moon.

Name: _____ Date: _____

Write **up** two times.

_____ _____

_ _ _ _ _ _ _ _ _ _ _ _ _ _ _ _ _ _

_____ _____

Draw a line from each frog to the lily pad that has **up**.

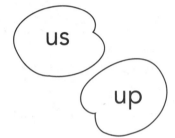

us

up

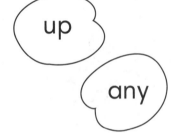

up

any

up

go

Write **up** on each spaceship.

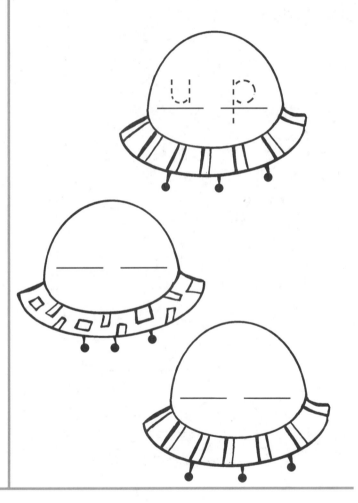

Color each computer that has **up**. Use yellow.

go   up   up   us   up

Name: _____   Date: _____

 look

Trace **look** two times. Use red, then blue.

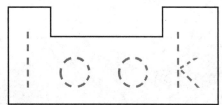

Color each space that has **look**. Use gray.

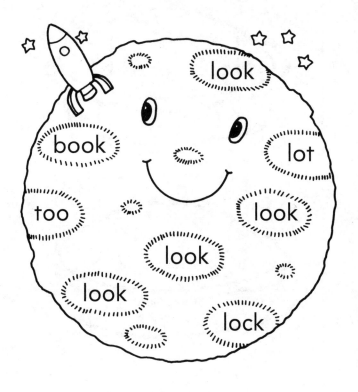

Read. Circle each **look**.

You can look for the moon.

You can look for the stars.

Just look up at night.

You don't have to look far.

Write **look** to complete each sentence.

I like to _____ at this book.

Come _____ at the squirrel.

Name: _____ Date: _____

Write **look**.

_____

_ _ _ _ _ _ _ _ _ _ _ _ _ _ _ _ _

_____

Connect the dots to spell **look**.
Find the word two times.

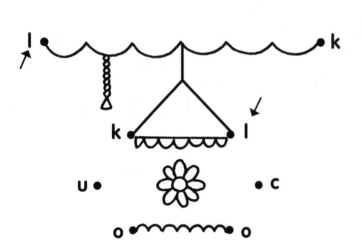

Write the missing letters
to spell **look**.

l _ _ k

_ _ o k

Color the glasses that have **look** on both sides. Use blue.

Name: _____ Date: _____

 **is**

Trace **is** two times. Use red, then blue.

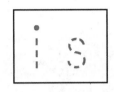

Help the bee find its hive.
Color each flower that has **is**.
Use purple.

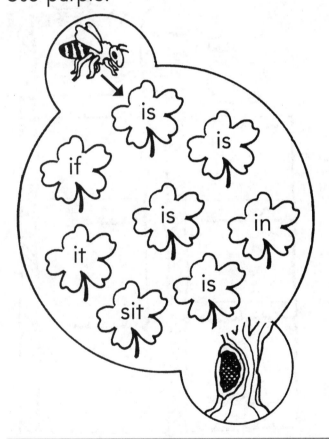

Read. Circle each **is**.

Here is a flower.

Here is a bee.

Where is the hive?

It is in the tree!

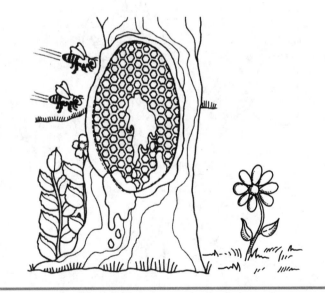

Write **is** to complete each sentence.

This ring _____ for you.

Milk _____ good for me.

Name: _____   Date: _____

Write **is** two times.

_____   _____

_____   _____

_____   _____

Color each pair of jellybeans
with the letters that spell **is**.
Use red.

Write **is** on each block.

Color each part of the snake that has **is**. Use orange.

is   is   us   is   as   is   is

Name: _____   Date: _____

Trace **go** two times. Use red, then blue.

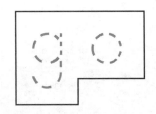

Color each fish that has **go**.
Use yellow.

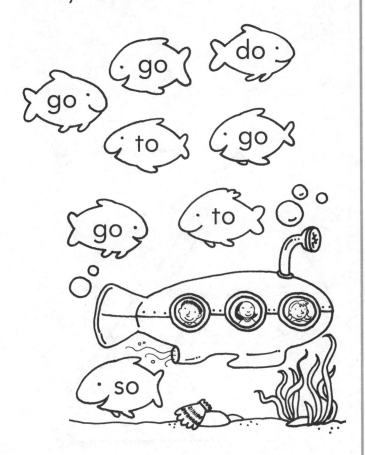

Read. Circle each **go**.

The fish go up.

The fish go down.

The fish go all around.

All the fish go and go,

but do not make a sound.

Write **go** to complete each sentence.

The car can _____ very fast!

We will _____ to the park today.

Name: _____ Date: _____

go

Write **go** two times.

_____ _____

_____ _____

_____ _____

Find each cup that has **go**.
Trace the path from that cup
to the teapot.

Write **go** on each pyramid.

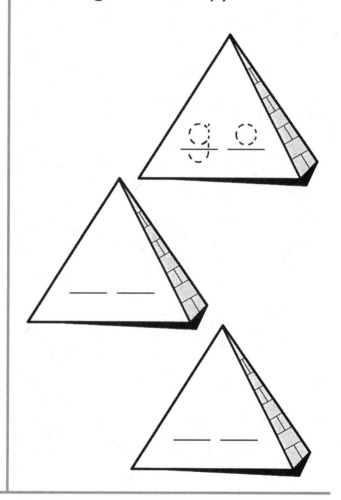

Color each tree that has **go**. Use green.

Name: _____ Date: _____

we

Trace **we** two times. Use red, then blue.

Color each cupcake that has **we**.
Use purple.

Read. Circle each **we**.

Can we have cupcakes?

Can we have cake?

Can we have pie?

It's time to bake!

Write **we** to complete each sentence.

Mom said _____ will ride the bus.

When do _____ get ice cream?

Name: _____   Date: _____

we

Write **we** two times.

_____   _____

_____   _____

_____   _____

Find each mushroom that has **we**.
Trace the path from that mushroom
to the mouse.

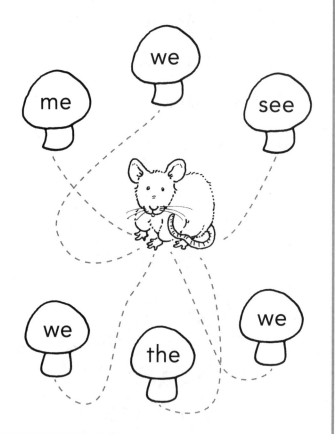

Write **we** on each clover.

Color each pair of friends with the letters that spell **we**. Use red.

Name: _____ Date: _____

little

Trace **little** two times. Use red, then blue.

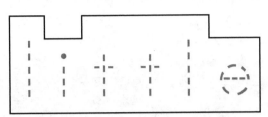

Color each space that has **little**. Use yellow.

little

like   live

little   little

light   tell

little   little

Read. Circle each **little**.

One little bee flew here.

Two little bees flew there.

Three little bees flew where?

To the little hive down there!

Bzzz, bzzz, bzzz.

Write **little** to complete each sentence.

The _____ mouse ran away.

I have a _____ book.

Name: _____   Date: _____

little

Write **little**.

_____

- - - - - - - - - - - - - - - - -

_____

Circle each **little**.
Find the word five times.

t l i f e t c
l i t t l e f
i t f c i l e
t t e j t f l
t l i t t l e
l e f t l c j
e t j c e i f

Color each balloon that has **little**. Draw a string from that balloon to the fence.

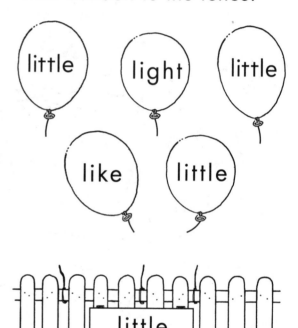

little   light   little

like   little

little

Help the chick get to the hen.
Trace the path with **little**.

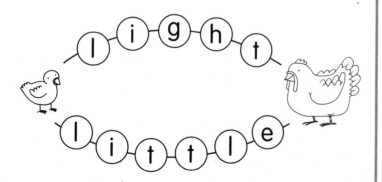

l i g h t
l i t t l e

Write the missing letters to spell **little**.

li __ __ le

__ i t t __ e

Name: _____   Date: _____

Trace **down** two times. Use red, then blue.

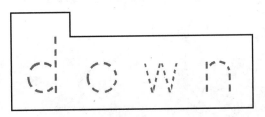

down

Help the kid get to the slide.
Color each space that has **down**.
Use green.

now   do   down

dig   down   now

know   two   down

down

did   who

down

down   don't

Read. Circle each **down**.

The leaves came down.

The rain fell down.

The birds flew down.

And I slid down!

Write **down** to complete each sentence.

Sit _____ on that stool.

I went _____ the stairs.

Name: _____ Date: _____

Write **down**.

_____

_____

_____

Help each raindrop get to the ground. Connect the dots to spell **down**. Start at **d**.

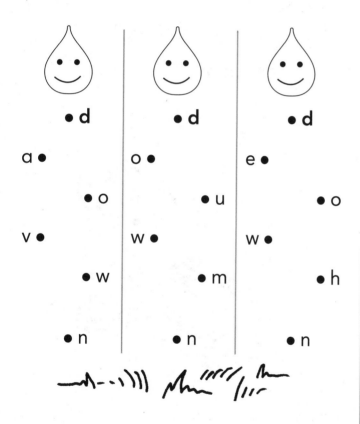

Write the missing letters to spell **down**.

do __ n

___ ___ w n

d ___ ___ ___

Color each bat with the letters that spell **down**. Use gray.

Name: _____ Date: _____

can

Trace **can** two times. Use red, then blue.

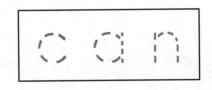

Color each ball that has **can**. Use purple.

Read. Circle each **can**.

What can you kick?

What can you throw?

What can you catch?

Tell me if you know.

You can do them all

with a big, round ball!

Write **can** to complete each sentence.

Look, I _____ jump!

We _____ go to lunch now.

Name: _____ Date: _____

Write **can**.

_____

- - - - - - - - - - - - - - - - - - - -

_____

Circle each **can**.
Find the word five times.

c	a	n	v
a	m	e	c
n	o	h	a
w	e	c	r
u	c	a	n
c	a	n	g
o	m	v	u

Write the missing letters
to spell **can**.

c __ n

__ a n

__ a __

Color the set of friends with the letters that spell **can**. Use blue.

The Jumbo Book of Sight Word Practice Pages © 2013 by Immacula A. Rhodes, Scholastic Teaching Resources • page 68

Name: _____ Date: _____

 **see**

Trace **see** two times. Use red, then blue.

Color each leaf that has **see**.
Use orange.

see me see she
so see
see saw

Read. Circle each **see**.

I look all around.

What do I see?

I see an owl!

Does it see me?

Write **see** to complete each sentence.

These glasses help me _____.

Do you want to _____ my fish?

Name: _____   Date: _____

Write **see**.

_____

- -

_____

Find each acorn that has **see**.
Trace the path from that acorn
to the squirrel.

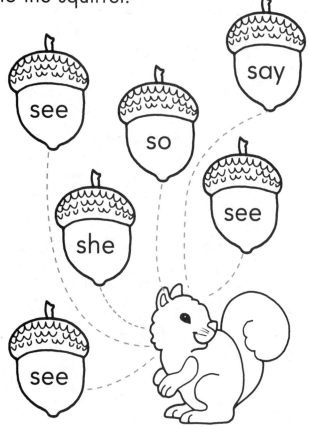

Write the missing letters
to spell **see**.

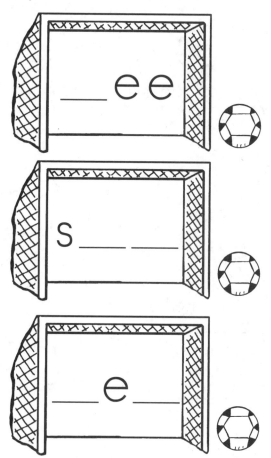

Color the two shoes with the letters that spell **see**. Use blue.

Name: _____   Date: _____

Trace **not** two times. Use red, then blue.

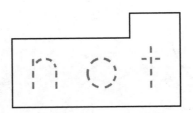

Color each stripe that has **not**.
Use red.

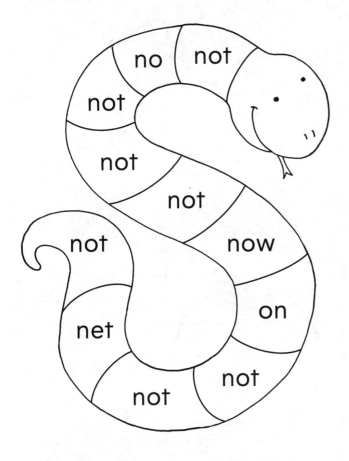

Read. Circle each **not**.

I do not run.

I do not fly.

I'm not much fun.

That is no lie.

I am not furry

from end to end.

But maybe you will

be my friend—or not!

Write **not** to complete each sentence.

We do _____ go to school today.

This is _____ my skate.

Name: _____ Date: _____

Write **not**.

_____

- - - - - - - - - - - - - - - -

_____

Help the mouse get to the cheese.
Trace the path that has **not**.

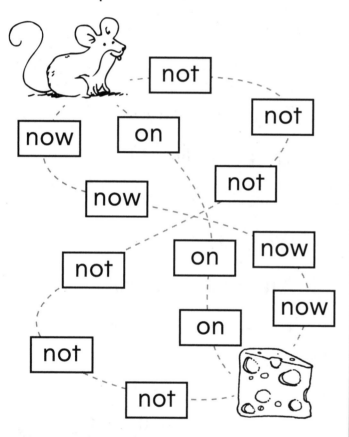

Write the missing letters
to spell **not**.

Circle each **not**. Find
the word five times.

m n o t e v
f o h u n a
e t a n o t
n o t m t h

Name: _____   Date: _____

 one

Trace **one** two times. Use red, then blue.

Color each firefly light that has **one**. Use yellow.

one   on   an   one   one   now   one   ran   one   once   won   one

Read. Circle each **one**.

This one little bug

makes one little light.

Now add one more,

and one more,

and one more,

and soon you will have

one big, bright light!

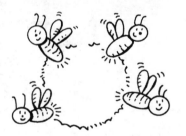

Write **one** to complete each sentence.

She gave me _____ cookie.

There is only _____ sun in the sky.

Name: _____ Date: _____

Write **one**.

_____

- -

_____

Find each pumpkin that has **one**. Trace the path from that pumpkin to the raccoon.

Write the missing letters to spell **one**.

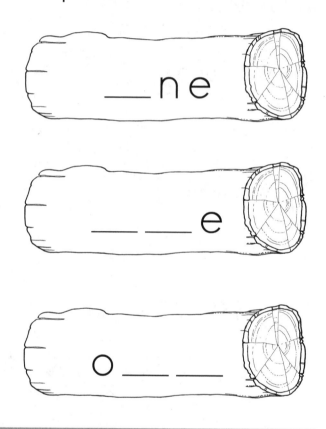

__ n e

___ ___ e

o ___ ___

Color each stack of blocks with the letters that spell **one**. Use red.

The Jumbo Book of Sight Word Practice Pages © 2013 by Immacula A. Rhodes, Scholastic Teaching Resources • page 74

Name: _____   Date: _____

Trace **my** two times. Use red, then blue.

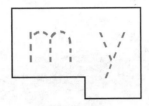

Color each gift that has **my**.
Use purple.

my	why
any	my
my	yes
my	me

Read. Circle each **my**.

Here are my candles.

Here is my cake.

Today is my birthday,

for goodness sake!

Write **my** to complete each sentence.

Have you seen _____ pencil?

Come look at _____ new bike!

Name: _____ Date: _____

Write **my** two times.

_____ _____

- -

_____ _____

Color each space that has **my**.
Use yellow.

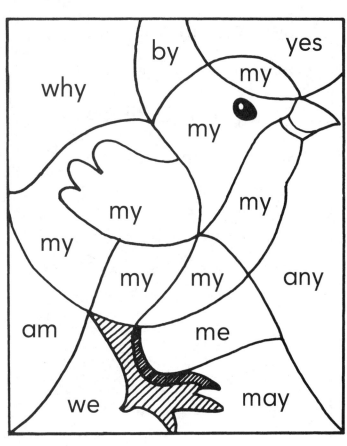

Write **my** on each bucket.

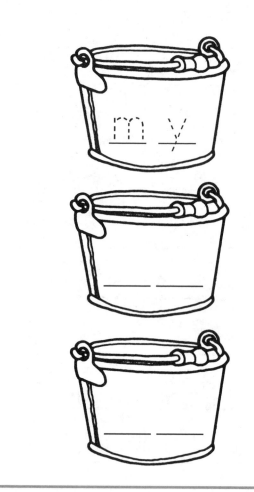

Draw a line from each bee to the hive that has **my**.

may my

my why

any my

Name: _____   Date: _____

me

Trace **me** two times. Use red, then blue.

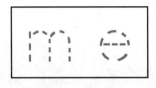

Help the labybug get to the flowers. Color each space that has **me**. Use brown.

men	me	may
my	me	me
the	she	me
he	me	me
	me	we

Read. Circle each **me**.

Look at me.

See me fly.

Look at me.

I fly so high.

Look at me.

See my spots.

Look at me.

I have lots!

Write **me** to complete each sentence.

Please make a sandwich for _____.

The man gave _____ a new top.

Name: _____   Date: _____

Write **me** two times.

_____   _____

- -

_____   _____

Find each berry that has **me**.
Trace the path from that berry
to the bear.

Write **me** on each fish.

Color each pair of music notes with the letters that spell **me**. Use red.

Name: _____ Date: _____

Trace **big** two times. Use red, then blue.

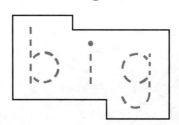

Help the bear get to the cave.
Color each space that has **big**.
Use yellow.

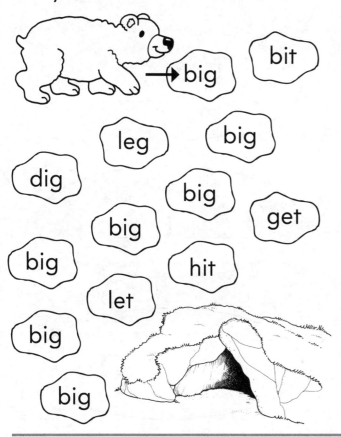

big bit
leg big
dig big
big get
big hit
let
big
big

Read. Circle each **big**.

Here is a big pillow.

Here is a big quilt.

Here is a big bed.

And here is a big,

sleepy bear.

Write **big** to complete each sentence.

I ride a _____ bus to school.

Dad gave all of us a _____ balloon.

Name: _____   Date: _____

Write **big**.

_____

- - - - - - - - - - - - - - - - - -

_____

Circle each **big**.
Find the word five times.

d	b	i	g
h	d	j	b
a	q	y	i
p	b	i	g
b	i	g	q
j	g	d	y

Write the missing letters
to spell **big**.

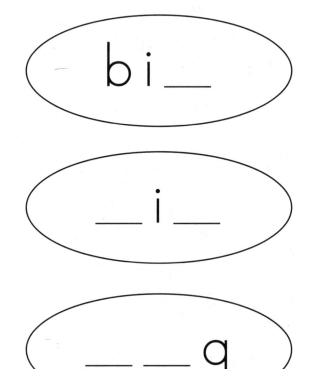

b i __

__ i __

__ __ g

Color each set of balls with the letters that spell **big**. Use orange.

Name: _____ Date: _____

come

Trace **come** two times. Use red, then blue.

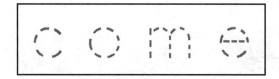

Help the kids get to the playground. Color each space that has **come**. Use green.

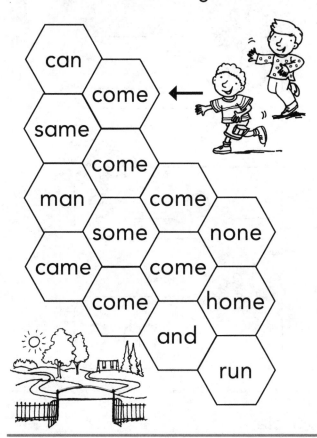

Read. Circle each **come**.

You can come

to the playground.

You can come to the slide.

You can come to the seesaw.

You can come to the duck

and ride.

Write **come** to complete each sentence.

Please _____ look at my turtle.

You can _____ to our house.

Name: _____ Date: _____

come

Write **come**.

_____

- - - - - - - - - - - - - - - - - - - -

_____

Circle each **come**.
Find the word five times.

s c o m e d
c a r c u n
o h v o w c
m c o m e a
e o w e h n
g m o c u e
a e g v m r

Write the missing letters
to spell **come**.

c o __ __

__ o __ e

__ __ m e

Color each robot that has **come**. Use purple.

some   come   home   come

Name: _____ Date: _____

Trace **blue** two times. Use red, then blue.

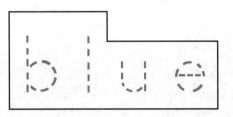

Color each bird that has **blue**. Use blue.

Read. Circle each **blue**.

A little blue bird,

up in the blue sky,

waved his blue wing

as a blue jet went by.

Write **blue** to complete each sentence.

The man was in a _____ car.

I want to wear my _____ shoes.

Name: _____   Date: _____

Write **blue**.

_____

_____

_____

Help the pig get to its ribbon.
Trace the path that has **blue**.

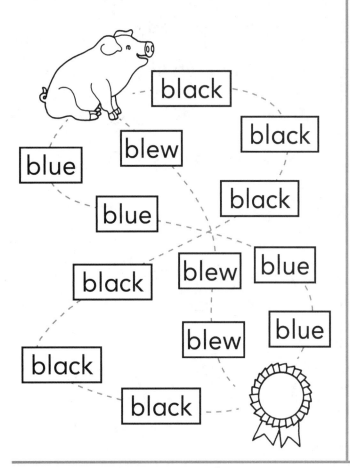

black
blew   black
blue
blue   black
black   blew   blue
blew   blue
black
black

Write the missing letters
to spell **blue**.

b ___ e

___ l u ___

___ ___ ___ e

Color each pair of clouds with the letters that spell **blue**. Use blue.

bl
ew

bl
ue

gl
ue

bl
ue

Name: _____ Date: _____

Trace **red** two times. Use red, then blue.

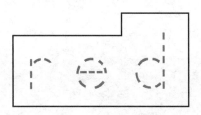

Color each apple that has **red**.
Use red.

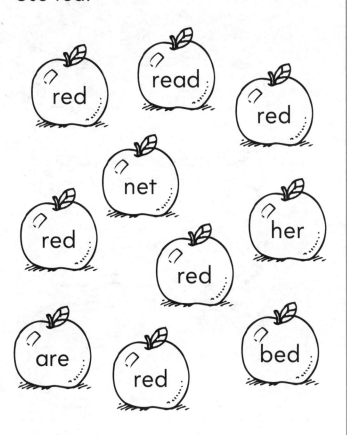

Read. Circle each **red**.

I have red hair on my head

and red shoes on my feet.

I have a red apple

in my hand—

a yummy food to eat!

Write **red** to complete each sentence.

The _____ bird has a nest.

He lives in a _____ house.

Name: _____   Date: _____

red

Write **red**.

_____

- -

_____

Connect the dots to spell **red**.
Find the word two times.

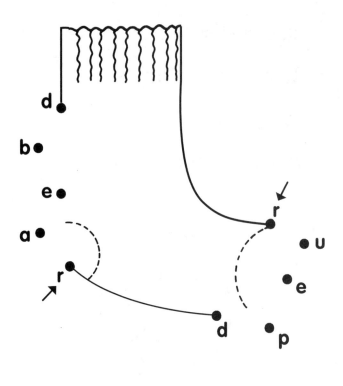

Write the missing letters to spell **red**.

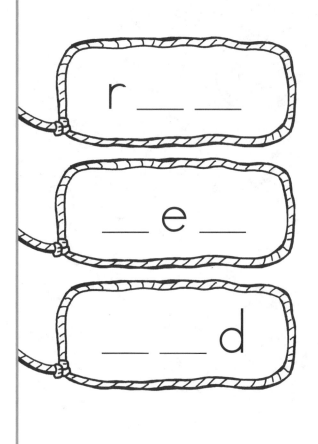

r _ _ _

_ _ e _

_ _ _ d

Color each pair of cows with the letters that spell **red**. Use red.

re   ad   re   d   ne   ed   r   ed

Name: _____ Date: _____

where

Trace **where** two times. Use red, then blue.

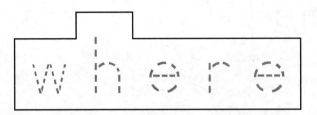

w h e r e

Help the dog get home. Color each space that has **where**. Use yellow.

where	where	here
when	there	where	she
where	where	where	when
where	here	we	went
where	where	where	

Read. Circle each **where**.

Oh where, oh where,

has my little dog gone?

Oh where, oh where,

can he be?

His tail is short

and his ears are long.

Oh where, oh where,

can he be?

Write **where** to complete each sentence.

I know _____ your shoes are!

Put the cup _____ it belongs.

Name: _____ Date: _____

where

Write **where**.

_____

- - - - - - - - - - - - - - - - - -

_____

Circle each **where**.
Find the word five times.

w	h	e	r	e	b	u
d	e	m	a	v	o	w
u	r	e	w	n	e	h
y	b	w	h	e	r	e
o	n	r	e	d	y	r
v	d	a	r	u	m	e
n	w	h	e	r	e	b

Color each ice-cream scoop that has **where**. Draw a line from that scoop to a cone.

when   where

where

where   there

Help the spider get to the web.
Trace the path with **where**.

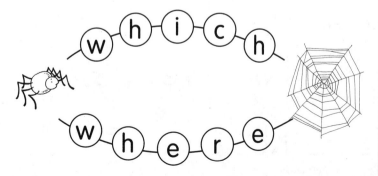

w h i c h h

w h e r e

Write the missing letters to spell **where**.

w h __ __ e

__ h __ r __

Name: _____ Date: _____

jump

Trace **we** two times. Use red, then blue.

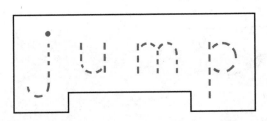

Help the grasshopper get to the rock. Color each grass patch that has **jump**. Use green.

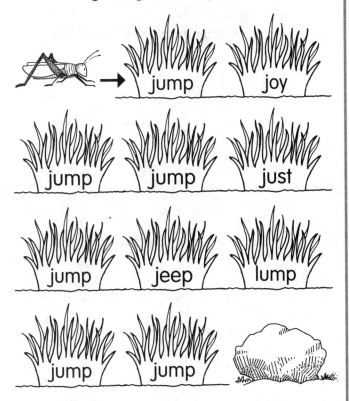

Read. Circle each **jump**.

A rabbit can jump.

A grasshopper can jump.

Now, look at me.

I can jump!

Write **jump** to complete each sentence.

Can a cow _____ over the moon?

I can _____ down the stairs.

Name: _____ Date: _____

jump

Write **jump**.

_____

- - - - - - - - - - - - - - - - - - -

_____

Find each frog that has **jump**.
Trace its path to the water.

Write the missing letters
to spell **jump**.

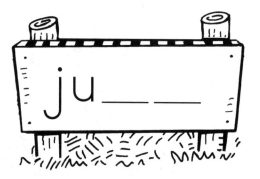

ju_____

___u___p

Color each pair of trees with the letters that spell **jump**. Use green.

ju mp

ju nk

ju st

ju mp

Name: _____ Date: _____

Trace **away** two times. Use red, then blue.

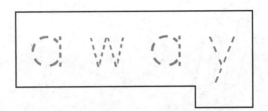

Help the cat get to the mouse.
Trace the path that has **away**.

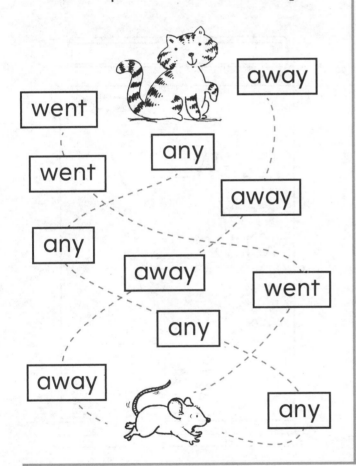

Read. Circle each **away**.

The mouse ran away

from the cat.

The cat ran away

from the dog.

The dog ran away

from me.

And I ran away

from the bee!

Write **away** to complete each sentence.

The train went far _____.

Stay _____ from the hot fire.

Name: _____   Date: _____

Write **away**.

_____

- -

_____

Circle each **away**.
Find the word five times.

m a g e w a

a w a y v w

j a w u n a

o y a w a y

v u y m q w

Write the missing letters
to spell **away**.

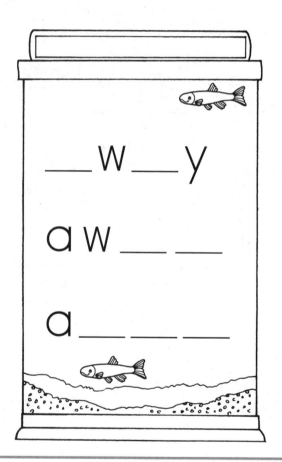

__ w __ y

a w __ __ __

a __ __ __ __

Color each fish bowl that has **away**. Use blue.

 way

 away

 want

 away

 away

Name: _____ Date: _____

Trace **here** two times. Use red, then blue.

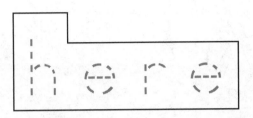

Color each leaf that has **here**.
Use yellow.

Read. Circle each **here**.

Red leaves are falling here.

Yellow leaves are falling here.

Brown leaves are falling here.

Look all around.

Fall is here!

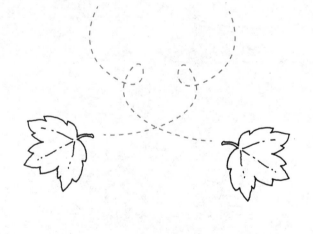

Write **here** to complete each sentence.

The mail is _____ now.

Put the paper _____ on the desk.

Name: _____   Date: _____

Write **here**.

_____

- - - - - - - - - - - - - - - - - - - -

_____

Find each boat that has **here**. Trace the path from that boat to the dock.

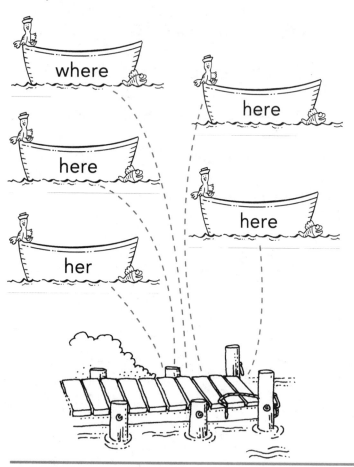

Write the missing letters to spell **here**.

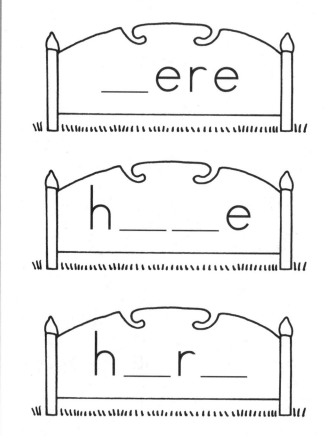

__ e r e

h ___ e

h __ r __

Color each flower with the letters that spell **here**. Use yellow.

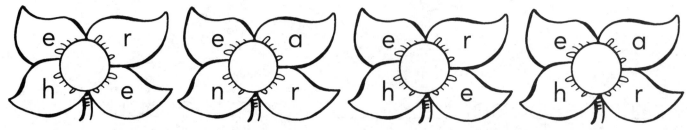

Name: _____ Date: _____

help

Trace **help** two times. Use red, then blue.

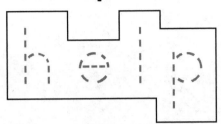

Help the kid get to the easel.
Color each space that has **help**.

she	here	hold
help	help	help	help
hat	put	hop	help
fell	her	the	help

Read. Circle each **help**.

Will you help me

draw a house?

Will you help me

draw a shoe?

Will you help me

draw a mouse?

Will you help me

draw you, too?

Write **help** to complete each sentence.

I will _____ clean the window.

Will you _____ rake the leaves?

Name: _____   Date: _____

Write **help**.

_____

- -

_____

Find each ball that has **help**. Trace the path from that ball to the basket.

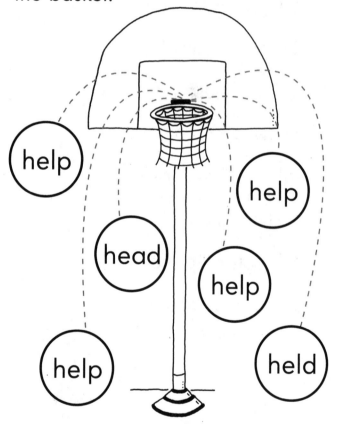

Write the missing letters to spell **help**.

__ e __ p

h e _ _ _

h _ _ _ _

Color the two puzzle pieces with the letters that spell **help**. Use orange.

Name: _____   Date: _____

make

Trace **make** two times. Use red, then blue.

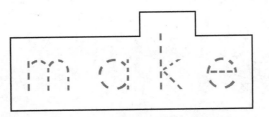

Color each space that has **make**. Use orange.

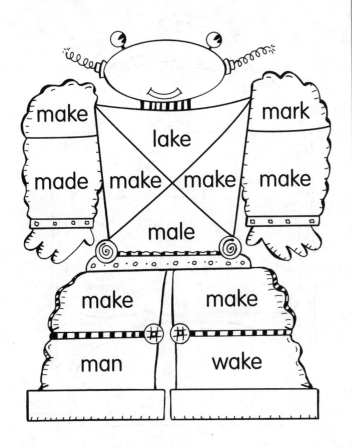

Read. Circle each **make**.

You can make a wish for me.

I can make a wish for you.

We can make a wish

together, then make a wish

that it comes true.

Write **make** to complete each sentence.

Let's _____ a pizza!

The spider can _____ a web.

Name: _____   Date: _____

Write **make**.

_____

- -

_____

Circle each **make**.
Find the word five times.

m a k e t u
a m a k e m
w a f o v a
u k c n t k
h e m a k e

Write the missing letters
to spell **make**.

m a ___ ___

___ ___ ___ k ___

Color each pair of cupcakes with the letters that spell **make**. Use pink.

Name: _____ Date: _____

Trace **yellow** two times. Use red, then blue.

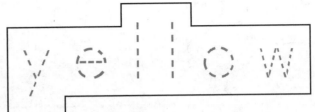

Color the signs that have **yellow**.
Use yellow.

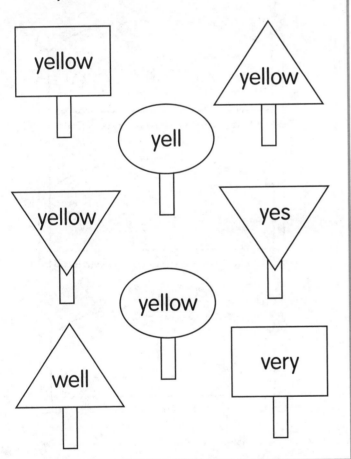

Read. Circle each **yellow**.

I put on a yellow shirt,

yellow pants,

and yellow shoes.

Then I walked through

some yellow leaves

to catch a yellow bus

to school.

Write **yellow** to complete each sentence.

These bananas are _____.

The _____ bunny is mine.

Write **yellow**.

_____

- - - - - - - - - - - - - - - - - - - -

_____

Connect the dots to spell **yellow**.
Find the word two times.

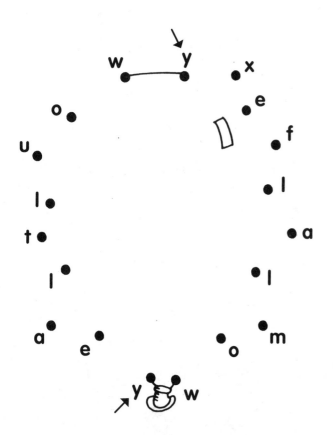

Write the missing letters
to spell **yellow**.

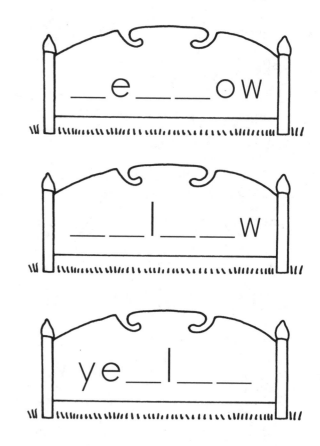

__ e __ __ __ o w

__ __ __ l __ __ w

y e __ l __ __

Color each chick that has **yellow**. Use yellow.

well   yellow   yellow   yellow   yell

Name: _____ Date: _____

Trace **two** two times. Use red, then blue.

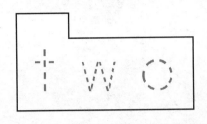

Color each balloon that has **two**. Use blue.

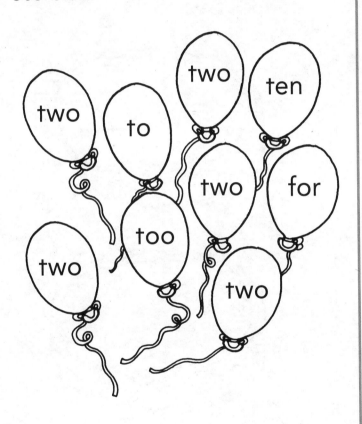

Read. Circle each **two**.

Bear has two ears.

Bear has two eyes.

Bear uses two paws

to hold two balloons.

Write **two** to complete each sentence.

I have _____ pencils.

These _____ mittens make a match.

Name: _____   Date: _____

Write **two**.

_____

- - - - - - - - - - - - - - - - - -

_____

Find each snail that has **two**.
Trace its path to the grass.

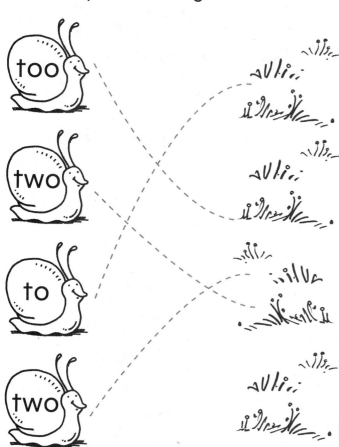

Write the missing letters
to spell **two**.

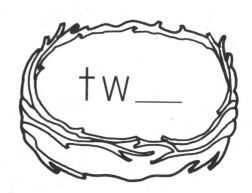

t w __

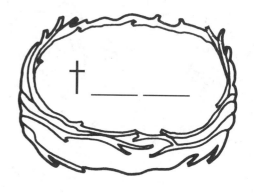

t __ __

Color each set of leaves with the letters that spell **two**. Use green.

play

Trace **play** two times. Use red, then blue.

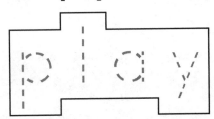

Help the kids get to their game.
Trace the path that has **play**.

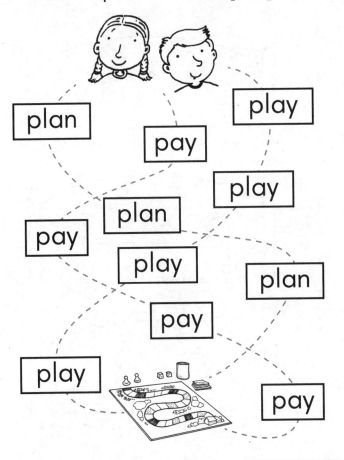

plan

pay

play

plan

pay

play

play

play

pay

plan

play

pay

Read. Circle each **play**.

I want to play a game.

I want to play with you.

You can play with

the red marker,

and I will play

with the blue.

Write **play** to complete each sentence.

I like to _____!

My friend can _____ the flute.

Name: _____ Date: _____

play

Write **play**.

_____

- -

_____

Connect the dots to spell **play**.
Find the word two times.

Write the missing letters
to spell **play**.

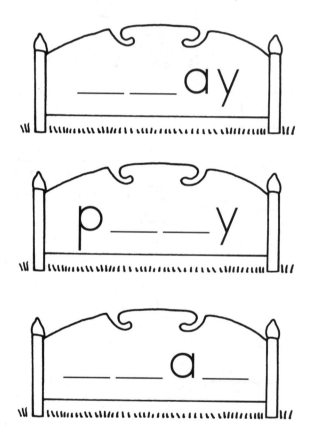

_____ a y

p _____ y

_____ a _____

Color each yo-yo that has **play**. Use orange.

 play  play  day  play  black

Name: _____ Date: _____

Trace **run** two times. Use red, then blue.

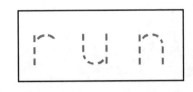

Color each bat that has **run**.
Use brown.

run

ran

am

run

run

are

Read. Circle each **run**.

Some people run

to win a big race.

Some people run to get fit.

Some people run

from place to place.

I run when I get a hit!

Write **run** to complete each sentence.

A deer can _____ fast.

I like to _____ to the barn.

Name: _____   Date: _____

Write **run**.

_____

- - - - - - - - - - - - - - - - -

_____

Help each cat get to its yarn.
Trace the path with **run**.

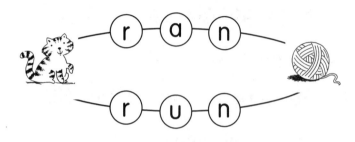

r a n
r u n

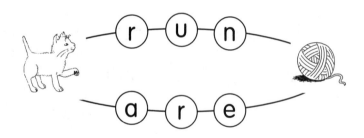

r u n
a r e

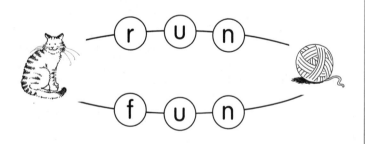

r u n
f u n

Write the missing letters
to spell **run**.

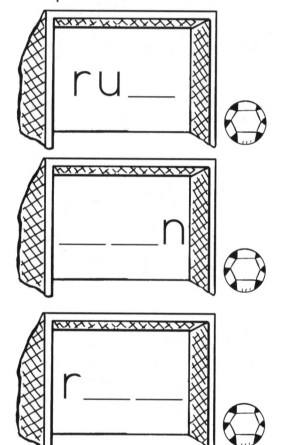

ru__

__ __ n

r _____

Circle each **run**.
Find the word five times.

m o w r u n
e r u n a r
r u n o v u
a n m r e n

find

Trace **find** two times. Use red, then blue.

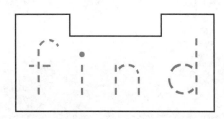

find

Color each ball that has **find**. Use purple.

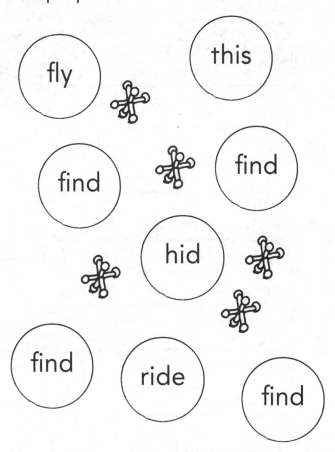

fly

this

find

find

hid

find

ride

find

Read. Circle each **find**.

I cannot find my jacks.

I cannot find my ball.

I cannot find my sack.

Will you help me

find them all?

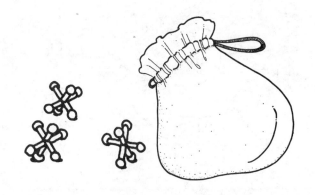

Write **find** to complete each sentence.

Did you _____ your hat?

Use a map to _____ the way.

Name: _____   Date: _____

Write **find**.

_____

_____

_____

Color each space that has **find**. Use yellow.

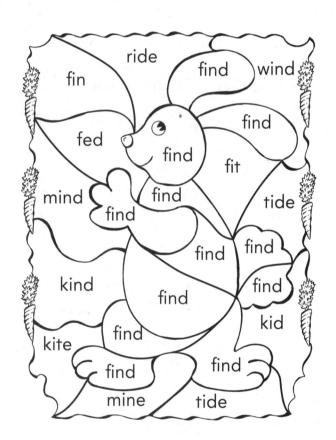

Write the missing letters to spell **find**.

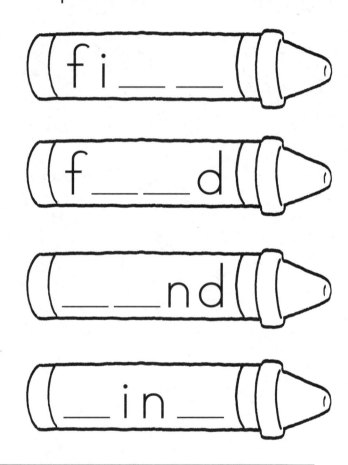

Color the glasses with the letters that spell **find**. Use green.

ki nd   mi nd   fi nd

fi nd   ri de

Name: _____   Date: _____

three

Trace **three** two times. Use red, then blue.

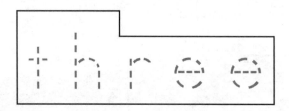

Color each train car that has **three**.
Use purple.

three | tree | here

free | three | three

three | there | three

Read. Circle each **three**.

Once, three little trains
went down the track.
The three left the station,
and the three came back.

Write **three** to complete each sentence.

Dad got out _____ cups.

We have _____ new fish.

Name: _____   Date: _____

three

Write **three**.

_____

- -

_____

Connect the dots to spell **three**.
Find the word two times.

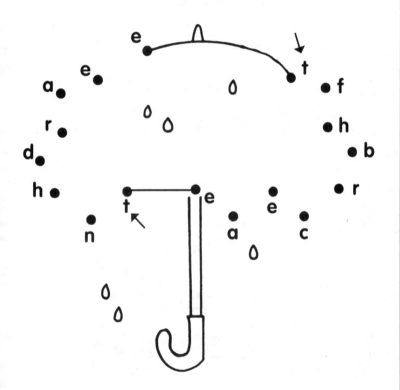

Write the missing letters
to spell **three**.

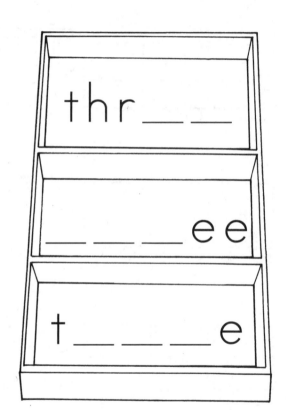

thr___

_____ e e

t_____ e

Color the boxes with the letters that spell **three**. Use orange.

f	h	n	c	u
t	n	r	a	e
k	m	w	e	g

l	n	w	u	e
f	v	r	e	c
t	h	m	g	a

Name: _____ Date: _____

funny

Trace **funny** two times. Use red, then blue.

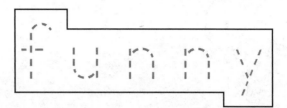

Color each hat that has **funny**. Use red.

Read. Circle each **funny**.

A funny little clown

in a funny hat

drove a funny car

until the tire went flat.

Now, that was funny!

Write **funny** to complete each sentence.

I just read a _____ book.

My friend has a _____ clock.

Name: _____   Date: _____

Write **funny**.

_____

- - - - - - - - - - - - - - - - - - -

_____

Find each spaceship that has **funny**. Draw a line from that spaceship to the alien.

Write the missing letters to spell **funny**.

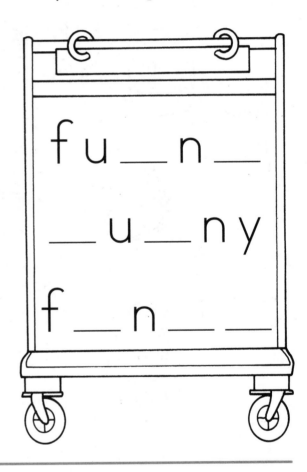

f u _ n _

_ u _ n y

f _ n _ _

Color each pair of peas with the letters that spell **funny**. Use green.

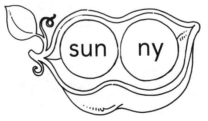

Name: _____   Date: _____

Trace **he** two times. Use red, then blue.

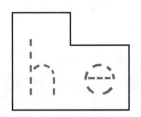

Help the sheep get to the gate.
Color each space that has **he**.
Use green.

Read. Circle each **he**.

Dad said he was tired,

and he wanted

to go to sleep.

So he got into his bed,

and he started

counting sheep.

Write **he** to complete each sentence.

It looks like _____ can jump.

The king sings as _____ swings.

Name: _____ Date: _____

Write **he** two times.

_____ _____

_____ _____

Color each space that has **he**.
Use orange.

Write **he** on each pyramid.

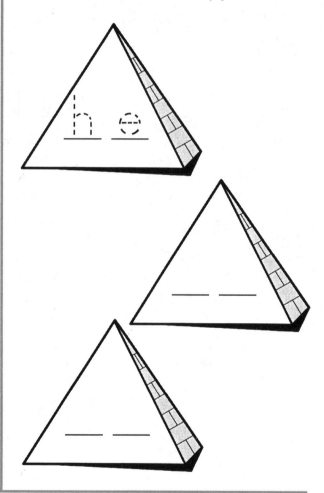

Color each pair of mushrooms with the letters that spell **he**. Use brown.

Name: _____   Date: _____

Trace **was** two times. Use red, then blue.

Color each space on the cake that has **was**. Use yellow.

Happy Birthday!

saw	say	yes
was	was	was
may	as	has
was	was	was

Read. Circle each **was**.

Today was great.

Today was fun.

Today was my birthday.

But now it's done.

Write **was** to complete each sentence.

The girl _____ asleep.

It _____ raining when I went out.

Name: _____ Date: _____

Write **was**.

_____

_____

_____

Help each bowling ball get to its pin. Connect the dots to spell **was**. Start at **w**.

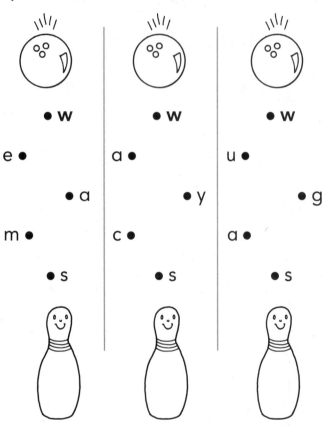

Write the missing letters to spell **was**.

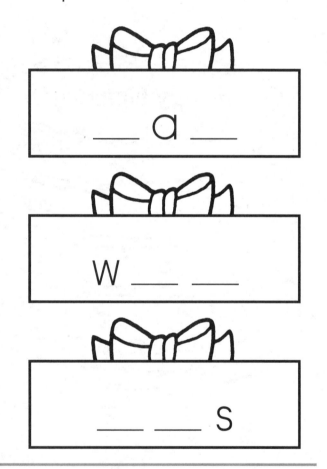

__ a __

W __ __

__ __ s

Color each set of candles with the letters that spell **was**. Use blue.

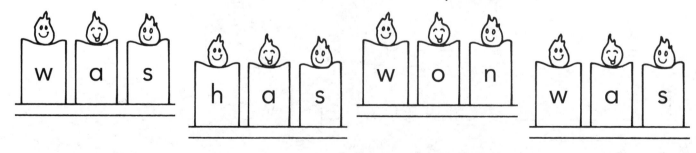

w a s   h a s   w o n   w a s

Name: _____ Date: _____

that

Trace **that** two times. Use red, then blue.

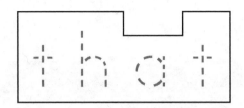

Color each fish that has **that**.
Use red.

Read. Circle each **that**.

I want to be a frog that jumps.

I want to be a bird that sings.

I want to be a fish that swims,

or maybe just a bee

that stings!

Write **that** to complete each sentence.

Can I have some of _____ gum?

We don't want _____ junk.

Name: _____   Date: _____

Write **that**.

_____

- - - - - - - - - - - - - - - - -

_____

Circle each **that**.
Find the word five times.

t n u f d e
h e t b o t
a f h u g h
t h a t u a
m o t h a t

Write the missing letters
to spell **that**.

t h ___ ___

t ___ ___ t

___ ___ a ___

Color each pair of apples with the letters that spell **that**. Use red.

th an   th at   th at   wh at

Name: _____ Date: _____

she

Trace **she** two times. Use red, then blue.

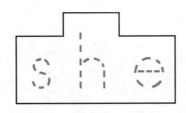

Find each flower that has **she**.
Trace the path from that flower
to the ladybug.

Read. Circle each **she**.

I know she has wings

and spots on her back.

I know she is red,

and her spots are black.

I know she likes leaves,

and she is nice as can be.

What is she, you ask?

A ladybug, you see!

Write **she** to complete each sentence.

The girl said _____ had a new ball.

I don't know why _____ is crying.

she

Write **she**.

_____

-- -- -- -- -- -- -- -- -- --

_____

Color each space that has **she**. Use purple.

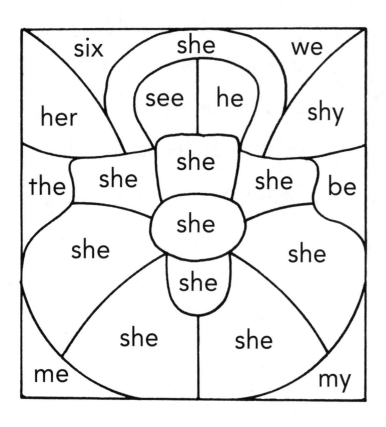

Write the missing letters to spell **she**.

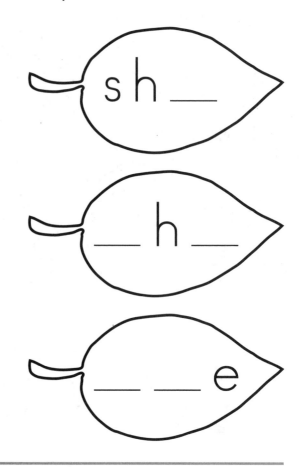

s h __

__ h __

__ __ e

Color each set of bags with the letters that spell **she**. Use green.

s h e

t h e

h e r

Name: _____ Date: _____

on

Trace **on** two times. Use red, then blue.

Help the fox get to the box.
Color each space that has **on**.
Use green.

on	on
in	only	won	on
an	on	on	on
of	on	and	now

Read. Circle each **on**.

The fox is on a box.

The cat is on a hat.

What is the frog on?

The frog is on a dog!

Write **on** to complete each sentence.

Turn _____ the lamp, please.

You can sit _____ this stool.

Name: _____ Date: _____

on

Write **on** two times.

_____   _____

_____   _____

Find each deer that has **on**.
Trace its path to the woods.

Write **on** on each bobsled.

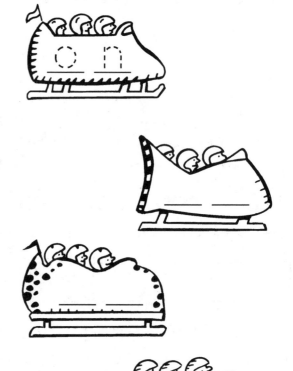

Color each part of the caterpillar that has **on**. Use blue.

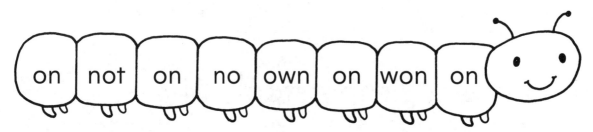
on | not | on | no | own | on | won | on

Name: _____   Date: _____

Trace **they** two times. Use red, then blue.

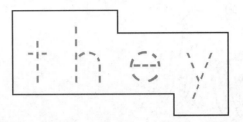

Help the duck get to the pond. Color each grass patch that has **they**. Use blue.

they	that
they	them
they	their	three
they	they	

Read. Circle each **they**.

Ducks do many things

that make me ask why.

Like why do they swim?

Why do they quack?

Why do they lay eggs?

And why do they fly?

Write **they** to complete each sentence.

Are _____ twins?

The coach said _____ could play.

The Jumbo Book of Sight Word Practice Pages © 2013 by Immacula A. Rhodes, Scholastic Teaching Resources • page 123

Name: _____   Date: _____

Write **they**.

_____

_____

_____

Circle each **they**.
Find the word five times.

c t h e y o
v u g t n t
f n o h a h
j t h e y e
t h e y x y

Write the missing letters
to spell **they**.

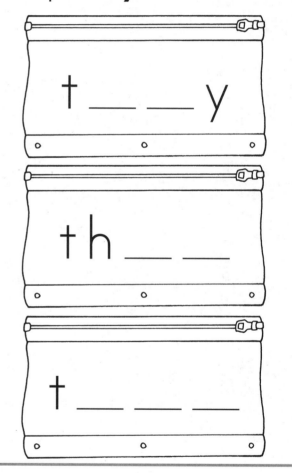

t __ __ y

t h __ __

t __ __ __ __

Color each pair of pears with the letters that spell **they**. Use yellow.

th ey

th em

th en

th ey

Name: _____ Date: _____

Trace **but** two times. Use red, then blue.

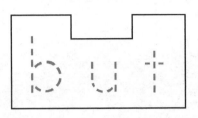

Color each snowflake that has **but**.
Use blue.

but by not

buy but

but

hot but nut

Read. Circle each **but**.

Snow fell one day,

but it melted away.

A snowbird came, too,

but it flew away.

Write **but** to complete each sentence.

The skunk is cute, _____ it smells.

He stayed outside, _____ it was hot.

Name: _____ Date: _____

but

Write **but**.

_____

- -

_____

Connect the dots to spell **but**.
Find the word two times.

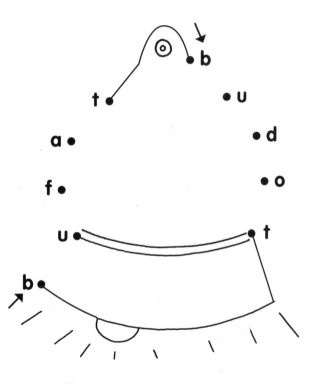

Write the missing letters
to spell **but**.

__ u t

b __ __

Color each banner that has **but**. Use yellow.

| buy | but | bug | but | nut | but | hut | but | hot |

Name: _____ Date: _____

Trace **at** two times. Use red, then blue.

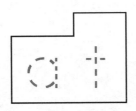

Color each elephant that has **at**.
Use brown.

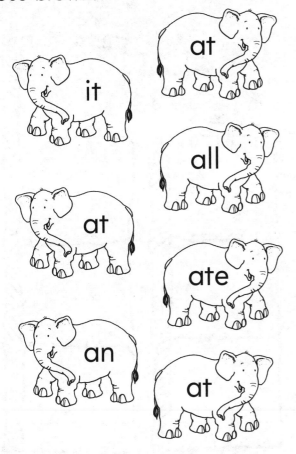

Read. Circle each **at**.

I saw an elephant at the zoo.

I saw a giraffe at the zoo.

And I saw you at the zoo, too!

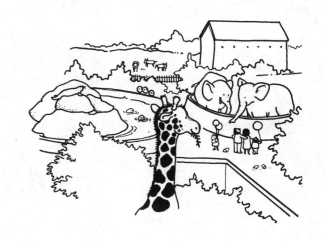

Write **at** to complete each sentence.

I left my bag _____ school.

We will meet _____ the park.

Name: _____   Date: _____

Write **at** two times.

_____   _____

_____   _____

Find each seal that has **at**.
Trace its path to the rocks.

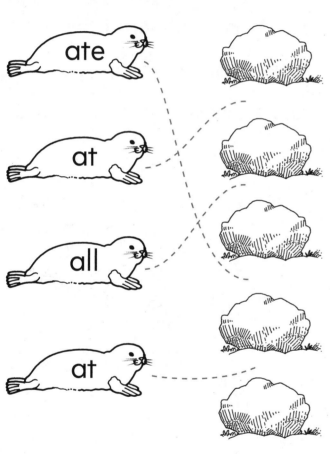

Write **at** on each block.

Color each bug with the letters that spell **at**. Use red.

Name: _____   Date: _____

with

Trace **with** two times. Use red, then blue.

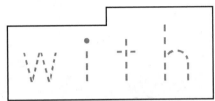

Color each cookie that has **with**.
Use yellow.

with   win

when

well   with

went

with   with

Read. Circle each **with**.

I like milk with cookies.

I like ice cream with cake.

I like to share with friends.

Join me, for goodness sake!

Write **with** to complete each sentence.

I brush my teeth _____ toothpaste.

You can build _____ my blocks.

Name: _____   Date: _____

with

Write **with**.

_____

- -

_____

Connect the dots to spell **with**.
Find the word two times.

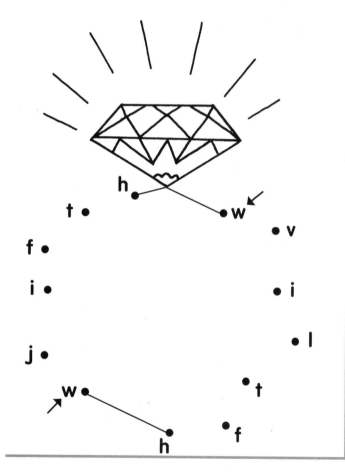

Write the missing letters
to spell **with**.

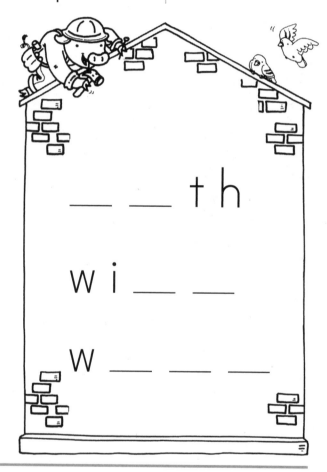

__ __ t h

w i __ __

W __ __ __

Color each pair of cookies with the letters that spell **with**. Use brown.

Name: _____ Date: _____

all

Trace **all** two times. Use red, then blue.

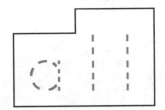

Color each spot that has **all**.
Use brown.

all   at   all

all   and   all   an

Read. Circle each **all**.

Cow has spots all over.

Giraffe has spots all over.

Frog has spots all over.

They all have spots!

Write **all** to complete each sentence.

I can ride _____ by myself.

Put _____ the crayons in the box.

Name: _____   Date: _____

Write **all**.

_____

- - - - - - - - - - - - - - - - -

_____

Help the worm get to the apple.
Trace the path that has **all**.

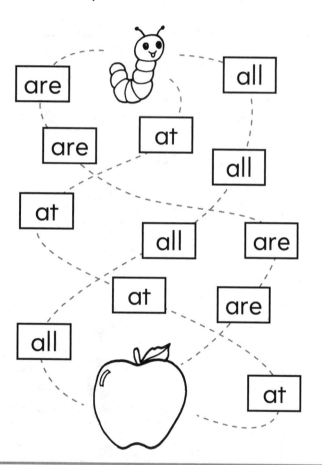

Write the missing letters
to spell **all**.

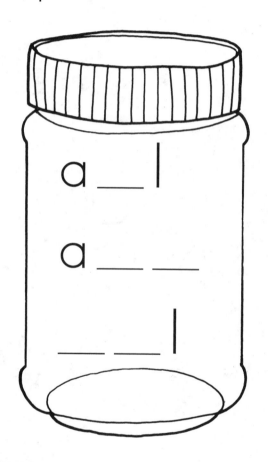

a __ l

a __ __

__ __ l

Color each car with the letters that spell **all**. Use purple.

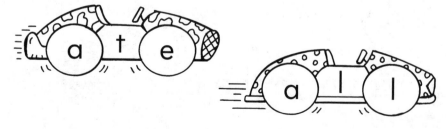

Name: _____ Date: _____

Trace **there** two times. Use red, then blue.

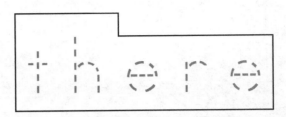

Color each space that has **there**. Use red.

Read. Circle each **there**.

Look over there!

See the house.

Look over there!

See the mouse.

Look over there!

The mouse is in the house!

Write **there** to complete each sentence.

The whale is out _____ in the sea.

My shoes are _____ by the door.

Name: _____ Date: _____

Write **there**.

_____

- -

_____

Circle each **there**.
Find the word five times.

f o t h e r e
u h a v l t b
d n t o e h r
c t h e r e f
h f e r u r b
l o r a v e k
t h e r e n d

Color each kite that has
there. Draw a string from
that kite to the kangaroo.

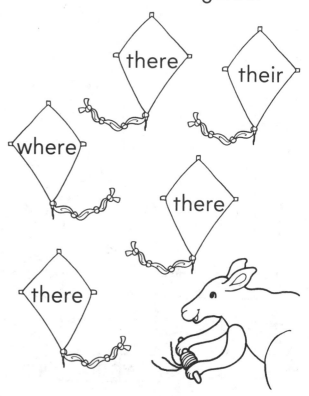

Help the lizard get to the rock.
Trace the path with **there**.

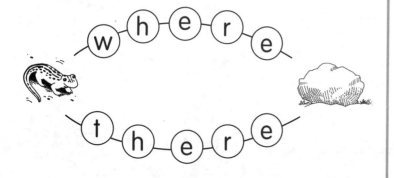

Write the missing letters
to spell **there**.

t h ___ ___ e

t ___ ___ r e

Name: _____ Date: _____

Trace **out** two times. Use red, then blue.

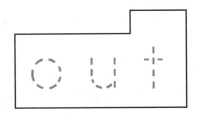

Color each space that has **out**.
Use purple.

out · out · but
not · our
eat · out
out

Read. Circle each **out**.

The dragon came out.

He stuck out his chin,

then puffed smoke

out of his nose.

Write **out** to complete each sentence.

The dog wants to go _____.

The boy went _____ for a run.

Name: _____ Date: _____

Write **out**.

_____

- -

_____

Help the rocket get to the moon. Color each star that has **out**. Use yellow.

Write the missing letters to spell **out**.

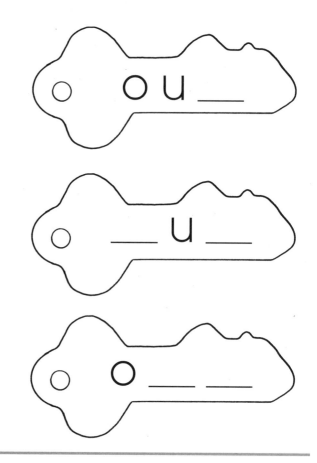

o u __

__ u __

o __ __ __

Color each set of balls with the letters that spell **out**. Use orange.

o   u   r

o   u   t

o   u   t

Name: _____   Date: _____

Trace **be** two times. Use red, then blue.

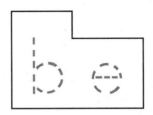

Color each tree that has **be**.
Use green.

Read. Circle each **be**.

If I could be a tree,

I would be as tall as can be.

But I can not be a tree,

so I will just be me.

Write **be** to complete each sentence.

Tim wants to _____ a funny clown.

The two girls must _____ twins.

Name: _____   Date: _____

Write **be** two times.

_____   _____

_____   _____

Help the train get to the track.
Trace the path that has **be**.

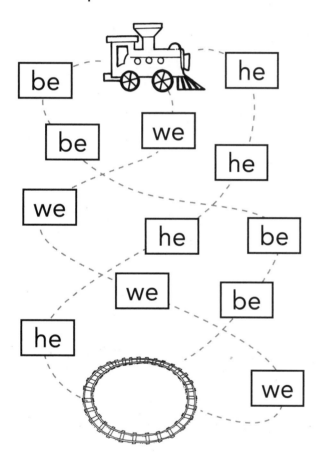

Write **be** on each duck.

Color each computer that has **be**. Use blue.

Name: _____ Date: _____

Trace **have** two times. Use red, then blue.

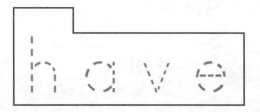

Color each plum that has **have**. Use purple.

Read. Circle each **have**.

We have apples.

We have plums.

We have bananas.

You can have some.

Write **have** to complete each sentence.

I _____ a loose tooth.

We _____ cake to eat.

Name: _____   Date: _____

Write **have**.

_____

_____

_____

Find each spider that has **have**.
Trace its path to the spout.

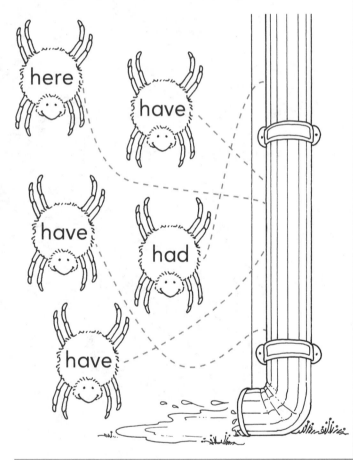

Write the missing letters
to spell **have**.

ha _____

h _____ e

_____ v _____

Circle each **have**.
Find the word five times.

h a v e w h
a r u b n a
v h a v e v
e n h a v e

Name: _____ Date: _____

 **am**

Trace **am** two times. Use red, then blue.

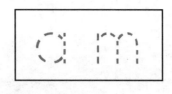

Color each space that has **am**.
Use gray.

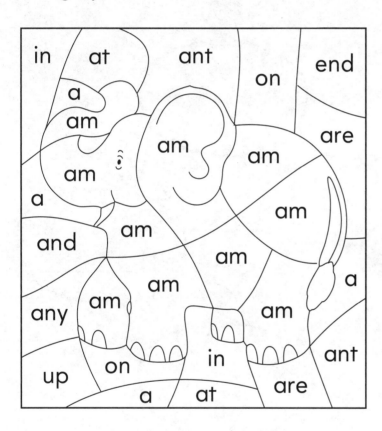

Read. Circle each **am**.

I am big.

I am gray.

I am at the circus

every day.

Write **am** to complete each sentence.

I _____ going to lunch.

I _____ happy!

Name: _____   Date: _____

Write **am** two times.

_____   _____

- - - - - - - - - - - - -   - - - - - - - - - - - - -

_____   _____

Find each cookie that has **am**.
Trace the path from that cookie
to the tray.

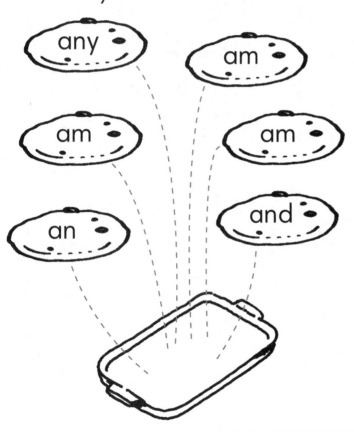

Write **am** on each bee.

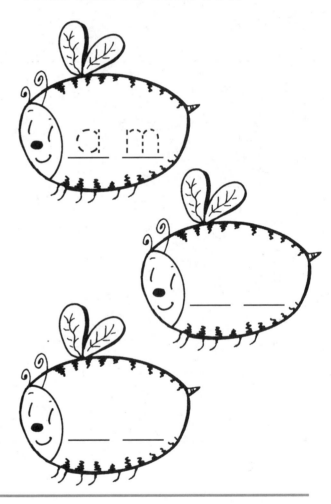

Color each pair of blocks with the letters that spell **am**. Use red.

Name: _____   Date: _____

Trace **do** two times. Use red, then blue.

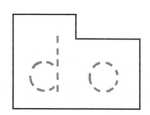

Color each space that has **do**.
Use brown.

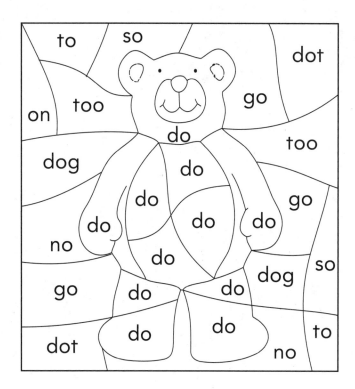

Read. Circle each **do**.

What do you want to play?

What do you want to do?

We can do what

you want to do.

Write **do** to complete each sentence.

What color _____ you like best?

I can _____ a flip!

Name: _____   Date: _____

Write **do** two times.

_____   _____

- -

_____   _____

Find each hippo that has **do**.
Trace its path to the water.

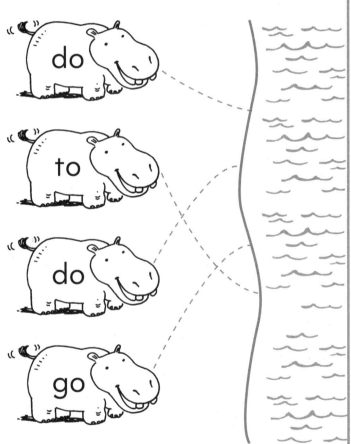

Write **do** on each tent.

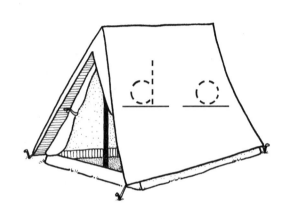

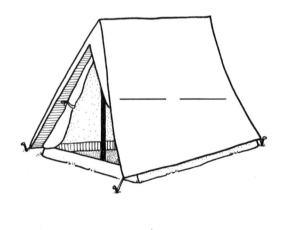

Color each pair of flowers with the letters that spell **do**. Use pink.

Name: _____   Date: _____

Trace **did** two times. Use red, then blue.

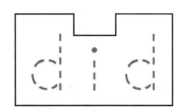

Color each banana that has **did**.
Use yellow.

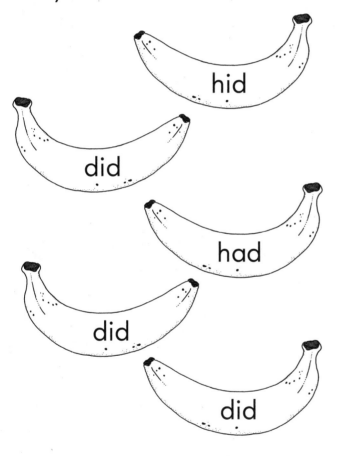

Read. Circle each **did**.

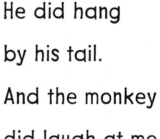

The monkey did

eat his banana.

He did go up

a tree.

He did hang

by his tail.

And the monkey

did laugh at me.

Write **did** to complete each sentence.

Dad _____ the dusting.

How _____ the pencil break?

Name: _____   Date: _____

Write **did**.

_____

- -

_____

Help the horse get to the hay.
Trace the path that has **did**.

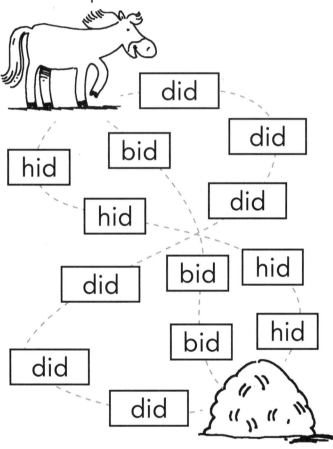

did

did

bid

hid

hid

did

did

bid   hid

bid   hid

did

did

Write the missing letters
to spell **did**.

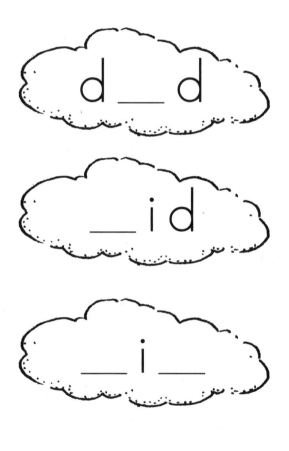

d __ d

__ i d

__ i __

Color each acorn that has **did**. Use brown.

 but    had    did    did    did

The Jumbo Book of Sight Word Practice Pages © 2013 by Immacula A. Rhodes, Scholastic Teaching Resources • page 146

Name: _____ Date: _____

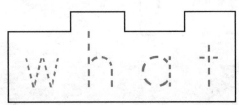

Trace **what** two times. Use red, then blue.

Color each space that has **what**.
Use orange.

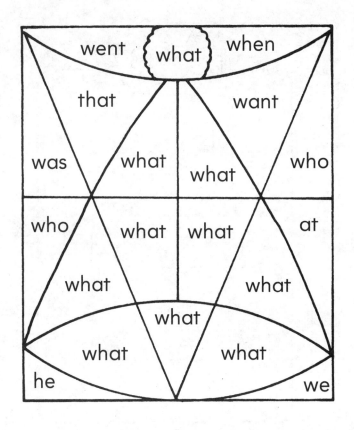

Read. Circle each **what**.

Look at what I did.

Look at what I made.

Look at what I drew—

a funny clown for you!

Write **what** to complete each sentence.

Do you know _____ time it is?

Tell me _____ animal has stripes.

Name: _____ Date: _____

what

Write **what**.

_____

_ _ _ _ _ _ _ _ _ _ _ _ _ _ _

_____

Circle each **what**.
Find the word five times.

v	d	e	f	w	u
w	h	a	t	h	w
h	f	n	v	a	h
a	e	b	u	t	a
t	u	w	h	a	t

Write the missing letters
to spell **what**.

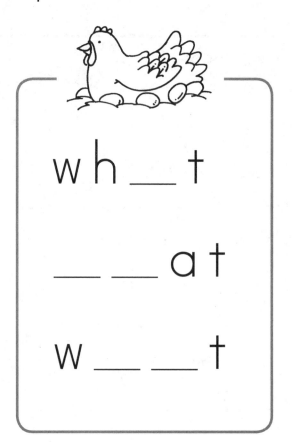

w h __ t

__ __ a t

w __ __ t

Color each clover with the letters that spell **what**. Use green.

Name: _____ Date: _____

 **so**

Trace **so** two times. Use red, then blue.

Color each turtle that has **so**.
Use green.

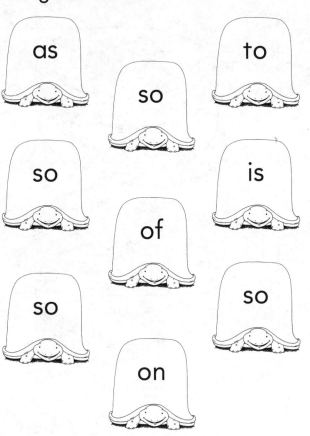

as | so | to
so | of | is
so | on | so

Read. Circle each **so**.

The turtle was so slow,

and the hare was so fast.

But the hare napped so long

that he finished last.

Write **so** to complete each sentence.

The boy said he was _____ cold.

Her hair is _____ long.

Name: _____ Date: _____

so

Write **so** two times.

_____   _____

- - - - - - - - -   - - - - - - - - -

_____   _____

Find each coin that has **so**. Trace the path from that coin to the bank.

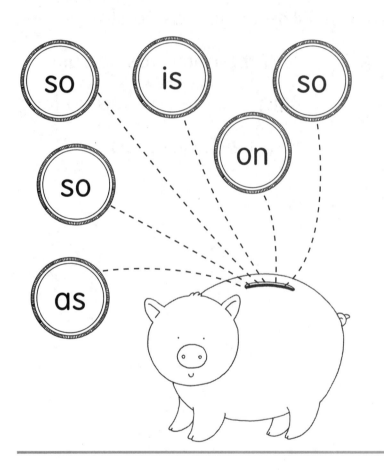

Write **so** on each yo-yo.

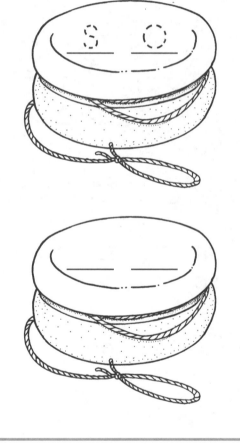

Color the two socks with the letters that spell **so**. Use blue.

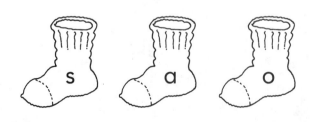

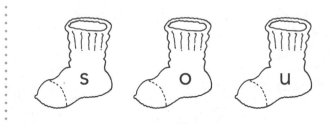

Name: _____   Date: _____

get

Trace **get** two times. Use red, then blue.

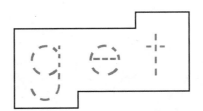

Help the boy get to the ball.
Color each space that has **get**.
Use brown.

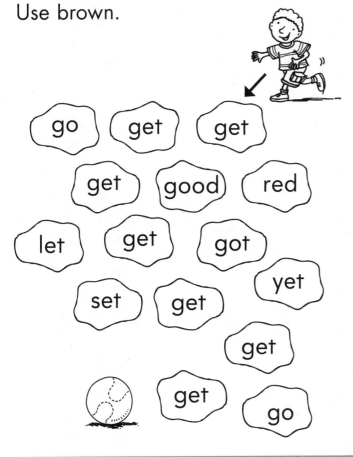

go   get   get

get   good   red

let   get   got

yet

set   get

get

get

go

Read. Circle each **get**.

Go get your bat.

I'll get my ball.

Then let's get our friends

to come and play ball.

Write **get** to complete each sentence.

Let's go _____ some ice cream.

I _____ to school on a bike.

Name: _____   Date: _____

Write **get**.

_____

_____

_____

Draw a line from each turtle to the puddle that has **get**.

 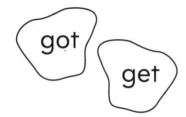
got   get

get   yet

set   get

Write the missing letters to spell **get**.

g e __

__ e t

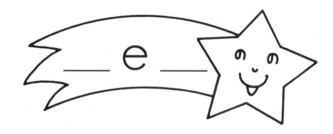
__ e __

Color each banner that has **get**. Use red.

| got | get | let | set | get | get | yet | get | go |

The Jumbo Book of Sight Word Practice Pages © 2013 by Immacula A. Rhodes, Scholastic Teaching Resources • page 152

Name: _____   Date: _____

like

Trace **like** two times. Use red, then blue.

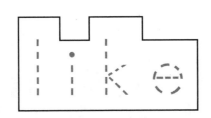

Color each space that has **like**.
Use yellow.

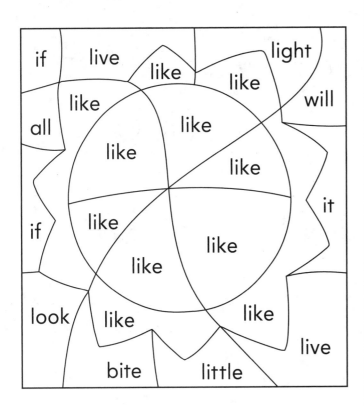

Read. Circle each **like**.

I like to jump.

I like to run.

I like to do flips

out in the sun.

Write **like** to complete each sentence.

We all _____ popcorn.

Do you _____ to paint?

Name: _____ Date: _____

Write **like**.

_____

_____

Help each giraffe get to its tree.
Trace the path with **like**.

ⓛ ⓘ ⓚ ⓔ

ⓛ ⓘ ⓥ ⓔ

ⓑ ⓘ ⓚ ⓔ

ⓛ ⓘ ⓚ ⓔ

ⓛ ⓞ ⓞ ⓚ

ⓛ ⓘ ⓚ ⓔ

Write the missing letters
to spell **like**.

_ i k e

_ _ k e

l i _ _ _

Circle each **like**.
Find the word five times.

l i k e f l
i l i k e i
k u r a j k
e t l i k e

Name: _____ Date: _____

Trace **this** two times. Use red, then blue.

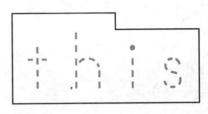

Color each book that has **this**.
Use yellow.

Read. Circle each **this**.

Put this stool

next to a light.

Then sit on the stool

to read this book.

Write **this** to complete each sentence.

Do you want to eat _____ apple?

Use _____ frame for your picture.

Name: _____   Date: _____

Write **this**.

_____

_- - - - - - - - - - - - - - - - - -_

_____

Connect the dots to spell **this**.
Find the word two times.

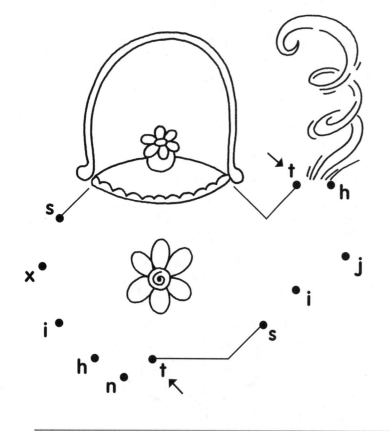

Write the missing letters to spell **this**.

Help the car get to the Finish line. Trace the path that has **this**.

thin	thin		thin		this	this		

this · this | | this | | thin | | thin |

FINISH

will

Trace **will** two times. Use red, then blue.

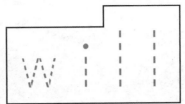

Color each space that has **will**.
Use red.

Read. Circle each **will**.

I will eat foods

that are good for me.

I will exercise

and brush my teeth.

I will get rest

and take care of me.

Write **will** to complete each sentence.

I _____ wash with soap.

When _____ we see a dinosaur?

The Jumbo Book of Sight Word Practice Pages © 2013 by Immacula A. Rhodes, Scholastic Teaching Resources • page 157

Name: _____   Date: _____

Write **will**.

_____

- - - - - - - - - - - - - - - - - -

_____

Draw a line from each snake
to the log that has **will**.

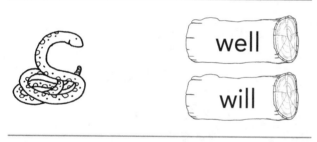

will

yell

well

will

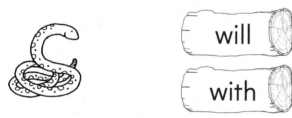

will

with

Write the missing letters
to spell **will**.

W i ____

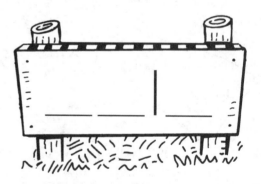

____ ____ I ____

Color each pig that has **will**. Use pink.

will   well   fill   will

Name: _____ Date: _____

 yes

Trace **yes** two times. Use red, then blue.

Color each pea that has **yes**.
Use green.

Read. Circle each **yes**.

We say yes to carrots.

We say yes to peas.

We say yes to corn

and yes to broccoli!

Write **yes** to complete each sentence.

Mom told us _____, we can play.

I say _____ to getting a cat!

Name: _____   Date: _____

Write **yes**.

_____

- - - - - - - - - - - - - - - - - - -

_____

Find each fish that has **yes**.
Trace its path to the water.

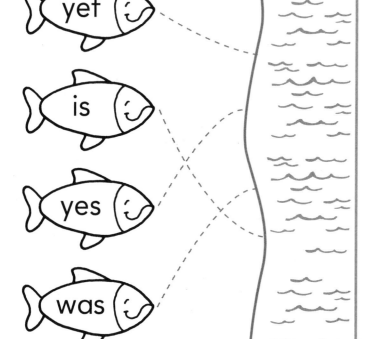

Write the missing letters
to spell **yes**.

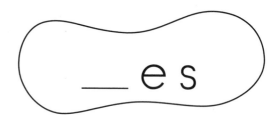

__ e s

y e __

y __ __ __

Color each flower with the letters that spell **yes**. Use yellow.

Name: _____ Date: _____

Trace **went** two times. Use red, then blue.

Help the family get to the other sidewalk. Color each space that has **went**. Use orange.

Read. Circle each **went**.

I went out.

My sister went out.

Dad went out.

Mom went out.

We all went out for a walk.

Write **went** to complete each sentence.

We all _____ to the store.

She _____ to sleep in her bed.

went

Write **went**.

_____

- -

_____

Circle each **went**.
Find the word five times.

m f y w a h
x o w e n t
k v u n d m
w e n t l x
e r f y x u
n l h a m k
t w e n t o

Write the missing letters
to spell **went**.

we _ t

W _ _ t

_ _ n _

Color each bat with the letters that spell **went**. Use gray.

wa   nt   we   nt   wh   en

Name: _____   Date: _____

Trace **are** two times. Use red, then blue.

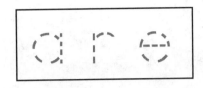

Color each space that has **are**.
Use use brown.

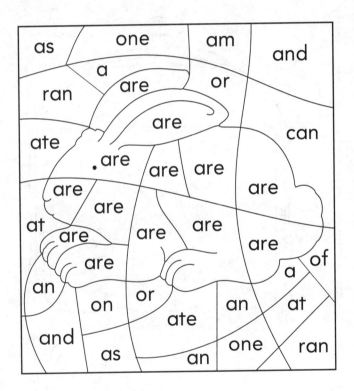

Read. Circle each **are**.

Rabbits are soft.

They are fun pets to keep.

Rabbits are quiet,

and they let you sleep.

Write **are** to complete each sentence.

They _____ running fast.

The boots _____ very wet.

Name: _____   Date: _____

are

Write **are**.

_____

- -

_____

Help each crow get to the corn.
Connect the dots to spell **are**.
Start at **a**.

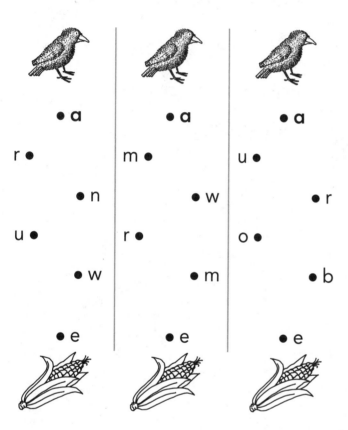

Write the missing letters
to spell **are**.

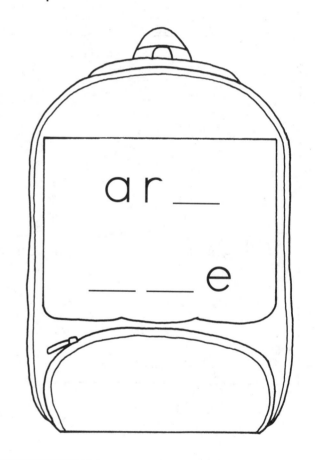

ar __

__ __ __ e

Color each train car that has **are**. Use blue.

are | ate | are | and | are

Name: _____ Date: _____

Trace **now** two times. Use red, then blue.

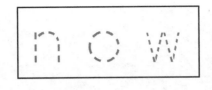

Help the cow get to the barn.
Color each grass patch that has
now. Use green.

how	new
now	now	one
no	now	not
won	now

Read. Circle each **now**.

Little cow, can you

stand now?

Can you walk now?

Can you run now?

Little cow, can you

moo now?

Moo!

Moo!

Write **now** to complete each sentence.

Let's have a snack _____.

It is raining right _____.

Name: _____ Date: _____

Write **now**.

_____

- -

_____

Circle each **now**.
Find the word five times.

m h a n
n o w o
u r d w
e n u v
h o m n
a w b o
v n o w

Write the missing letters to spell **now**.

n _ w

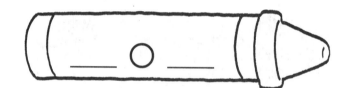
_ o _

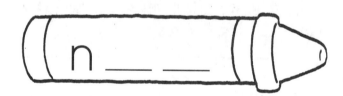
n _ _ _

Help the mouse get to the cheese. Trace the path that has **now**.

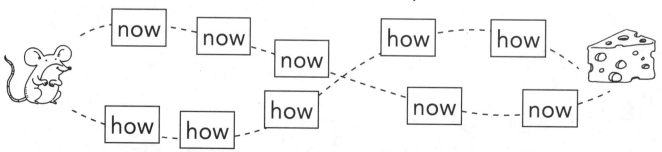

Name: _____ Date: _____

Trace **no** two times. Use red, then blue.

Help Jack and Jill get down the hill. Color each space that has **no**. Use brown.

Read. Circle each **no**.

Oh, no! Stay off that hill!

Oh, no! Look out, Jill!

Oh, no! Jack took a spill!

Write **no** to complete each sentence.

There is _____ milk in this glass.

One seal has _____ ball.

Name: _____ Date: _____

no

Write **no** two times.

_____   _____

_ _ _ _ _ _ _ _ _   _ _ _ _ _ _ _ _ _

_____   _____

Find each spider that has **no**.
Trace the path from that spider
to the web.

Write **no** on each clover.

Color each vest with the letters that spell **no**. Use blue.

Name: _____ Date: _____

Trace **came** two times. Use red, then blue.

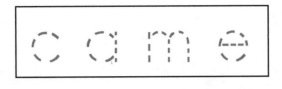

Color each school that has **came**.
Use red.

Read. Circle each **came**.

A firefighter

came to school.

A dentist came to school.

A chef came to school.

And our teacher

came to school!

Write **came** to complete each sentence.

My friend _____ over to play.

The rain _____ down hard.

Name: _____   Date: _____

Write **came**.

_____

- - - - - - - - - - - - - - - - -

_____

Help each bird get to its tree.
Trace the path that spells **came**.

Write the missing letters
to spell **came**.

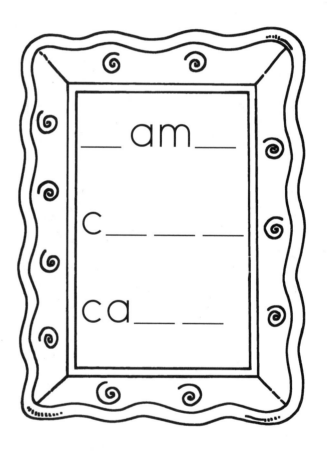

__ am __

c _____

ca _____

Color each fish bowl that has **came**. Use green.

come

came

came

can

name

Name: _____   Date: _____

Trace **ride** two times. Use red, then blue.

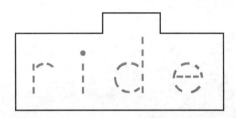

Color each train car that has **ride**. Use red.

Read. Circle each **ride**.

You can ride on a wagon.

You can ride on a train.

You can ride on a bike.

You can ride on a plane!

Write **ride** to complete each sentence.

Let's take a _____ in a cab.

I can _____ a horse.

Name: _____   Date: _____

ride

Write **ride**.

_____

_____

_____

Circle each **ride**.
Find the word five times.

p r a n k r
r i d e b i
a d k j p d
b e r i d e
n r i d e l

Write the missing letters
to spell **ride**.

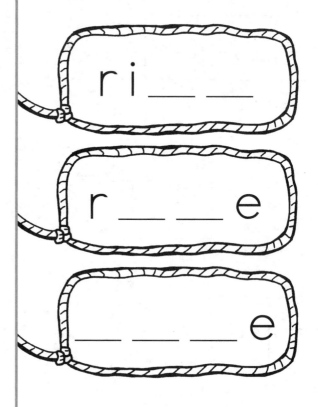

r i ___ ___

r ___ ___ e

___ ___ ___ e

Color each pair of cows with the letters that spell **ride**. Use orange.

ri de   hi de   re ad   ri de

Name: _____   Date: _____

into

Trace **into** two times. Use red, then blue.

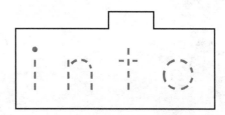

i n t o

Help the bear get to its bed.
Color each space that has **into**.
Use yellow.

into	not	in
out	into	into	its
sit	two	into	into
too	upon	do	into
on	is	win	

Read. Circle each **into**.

The bear went into his house.

He went into his room.

He got into his pajamas.

Then he got into his bed.

Good night!

Write **into** to complete each sentence.

The frog jumped _____ the water.

Let's go _____ that store.

Name: _____   Date: _____

Write **into**.

_____

_ _

Connect the dots to spell **into**.
Find the word two times.

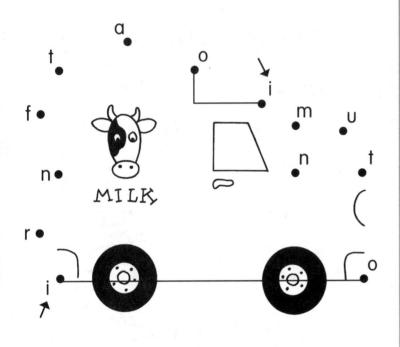

Write the missing letters to spell **into**.

in____

____ to

i____ o

Color the two puzzle pieces with the letters that spell **into**. Use green.

good

Trace **good** two times. Use red, then blue.

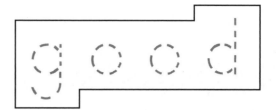

Color each ice-cream scoop that has **good**. Use brown.

Read. Circle each **good**.

Bananas are good.

Cherries are good.

Ice cream is good.

A banana split is good.

Yum! Yum!

Write **good** to complete each sentence.

These cookies taste _____.

The girl is a _____ skater.

Name: _____ Date: _____

Write **good**.

_____

_____

_____

Help each sheep get to its barn.
Trace the path with **good**.

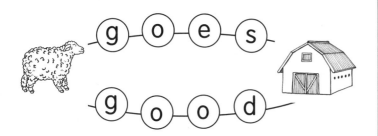

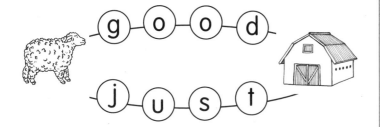

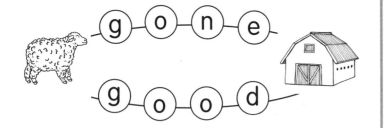

Write the missing letters
to spell **good**.

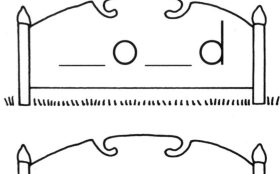

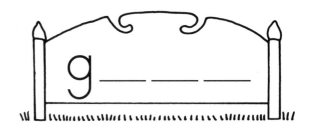

Color each bat with the letters that spell **good**. Use gray.

Name: _____ Date: _____

Trace **want** two times. Use red, then blue.

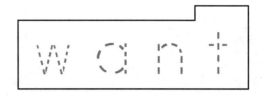

Color each popcorn bag that has **want**. Use red.

Read. Circle each **want**.

What do we want?

We want ice cream!

What do we want?

We want pie!

What do we want?

We want popcorn

piled up high!

Write **want** to complete each sentence.

Do you _____ some cake?

I _____ a pet turtle.

Name: _____ Date: _____

Write **want**.

_____

_____

_____

Circle each **want**.
Find the word five times.

c o w e m w

v w a n t a

w a n t v n

f c t m u t

o w a n t e

Write the missing letters
to spell **want**.

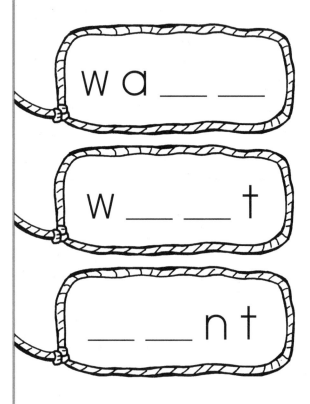

w a _____

w _____t

_____n t

Color each bear that has **want**. Use yellow.

went want want what with wish

Name: _____ Date: _____

Trace **too** two times. Use red, then blue.

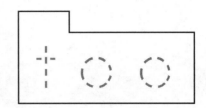

Help the pig get to the mud.
Color each space that has **too**.
Use brown.

two	too	log	ten
do	too	too	tin
to	top	too	tip
two	new	too	too

Read. Circle each **too**.

One pig left the barn.

The other pig did, too.

One pig played in the mud.

The other pig did, too.

One pig called out, "Oink!"

The other pig did, too!

Write **too** to complete each sentence.

The tea is _____ hot to drink.

It is _____ windy to play.

Name: _____   Date: _____

too

Write **too**.

_____

- - - - - - - - - - - - - -

_____

Find each fish that has **too**.
Trace its path to the water.

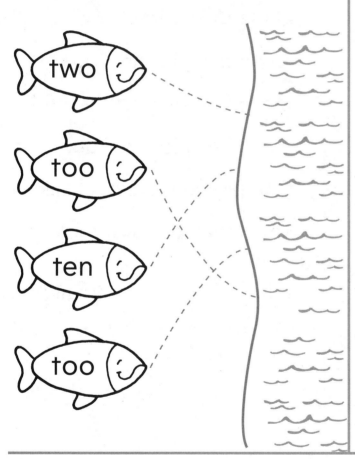

Write the missing letters
to spell **too**.

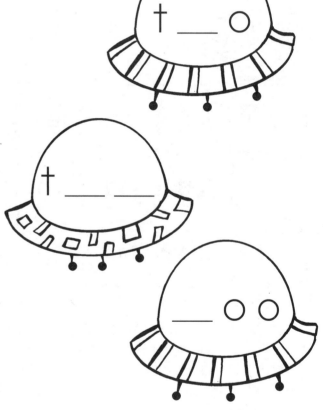

t __ o

t ___

__ o o

Color each part of the caterpillar that has **too**. Use blue.

too too two to too too ten do too too

Name: _____ Date: _____

pretty

Trace **pretty** two times. Use red, then blue.

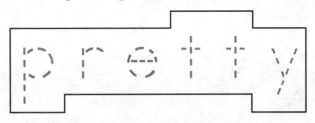

Color each bird that has **pretty**.
Use blue.

pretty

there

please

pretty

pretty

better

every

pretty

Read. Circle each **pretty**.

This pretty bird
learned to fly.
This pretty bird
left its nest.
This pretty bird
sits up high.
This pretty bird
sings its best!

Write **pretty** to complete each sentence.

The girl has _____ hair.

Here is a _____ quilt.

Name: _____   Date: _____

pretty

Write **pretty**.

_____

_ _

_____

Circle each **pretty**.
Find the word five times.

p	r	e	t	t	y	n
r	e	w	g	v	p	o
e	f	m	u	d	r	b
t	b	x	g	a	e	w
t	p	r	e	t	t	y
y	u	d	v	o	t	m
p	r	e	t	t	y	f

Color each ice-cream scoop that has **pretty**. Draw a line from that scoop to a cone.

Help the squirrel get to the tree.
Trace the path with **pretty**.

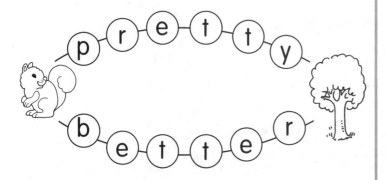

Write the missing letters to spell **pretty**.

p __ __ t __ y

__ __ e t __ __

Name: _____   Date: _____

Trace **four** two times. Use red, then blue.

Color each star that has **four**. Use yellow.

Read. Circle each **four**.

See the four stars.

Make a wish on all four.

If four wishes come true,

then good for you!

Write **four** to complete each sentence.

There are _____ peas in the pod.

We will be away _____ days.

Name: _____ Date: _____

Write **four**.

_____

- - - - - - - - - - - - - - - - - -

_____

Help each raindrop get to the ground.
Connect the dots to spell **four**.
Start at **f**.

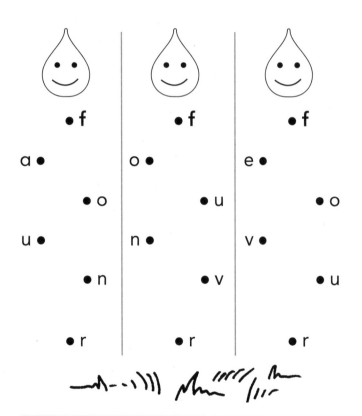

Write the missing letters
to spell **four**.

_ o u _

f _ u _

f _ _ _ r

Color each robot that has **four**. Use red.

four   your   four   from

Name: _____ Date: _____

saw

Trace **saw** two times. Use red, then blue.

Color each space that has **saw**. Use blue.

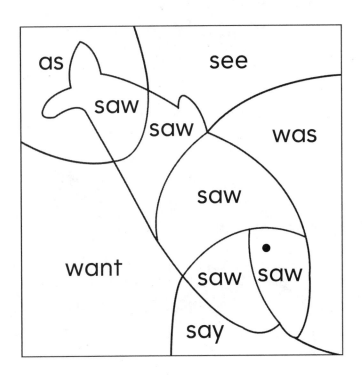

as
see
saw
saw
was
saw
want
saw · saw
say

Read. Circle each **saw**.

I saw a shark

out in the sea.

I saw a shark,

but he didn't

see me!

Write **saw** to complete each sentence.

We _____ a funny clown.

I _____ him catch the ball.

Name: _____ Date: _____

saw

Write **saw**.

_____

- - - - - - - - - - - - - - - - - -

_____

Circle each **saw**.
Find the word five times.

e	s	x	v
s	a	w	u
c	w	o	s
v	e	r	a
x	s	a	w
m	u	c	o
s	a	w	n

Write the missing letters
to spell **saw**.

__a w

s a__

__a__

Help the car get to the Finish line. Trace the path that has **saw**.

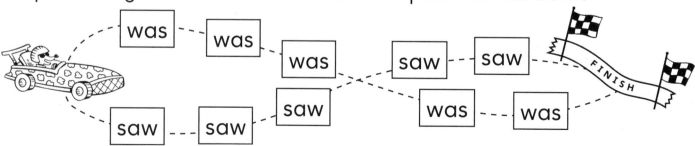

Name: _____ Date: _____

well

Trace **well** two times. Use red, then blue.

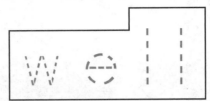

Help the car get to the doctor.
Color each space that has **well**.
Use red.

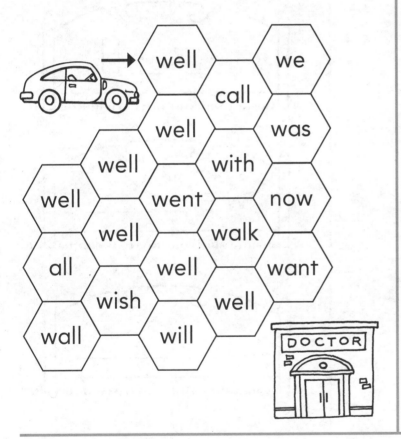

Read. Circle each **well**.

I feel well.

My dog feels well.

My cat feels well.

But my friend

does not feel well.

Write **well** to complete each sentence.

The girl paints very _____.

Oh _____, I made a mess!

Name: _____ Date: _____

Write **well**.

_____

- - - - - - - - - - - - - - - - - -

_____

Find each frog that has **well**.
Trace its path to the water.

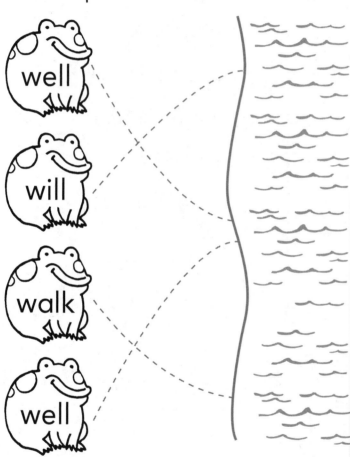

Write the missing letters
to spell **well**.

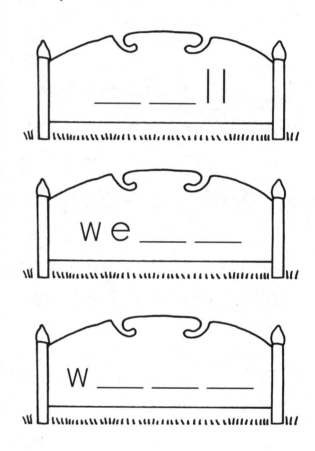

Color each pair of trees with the letters that spell **well**. Use blue.

Name: _____   Date: _____

ran

Trace **ran** two times. Use red, then blue.

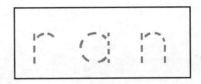

Help the runners get to the Finish line. Color each space that has **ran**. Use purple.

FINISH

an	was	ran	and
red	one	ran	any
won	ran	ran	run
ran	man	in	

→ ran

Read. Circle each **ran**.

We ran so long.

We ran so hard.

We ran so fast

that we ran

out of breath!

Write **ran** to complete each sentence.

He _____ to the store for Mom.

We _____ away from the skunk!

Name: _____ Date: _____

ran

Write **ran**.

_____

- -

_____

Connect the dots to spell **ran**.
Find the word two times.

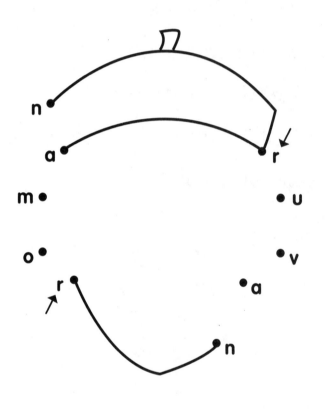

Write the missing letters
to spell **ran**.

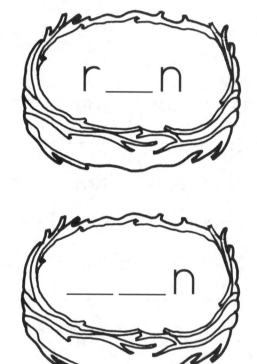

r__n

___ ___n

Color each owl that has **ran**. Use gray.

run and ran ran on ran one ran

Name: _____   Date: _____

 brown

Trace **brown** two times. Use red, then blue.

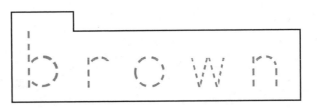

Help the horse get to the hay.
Color each space that has **brown**.
Use brown.

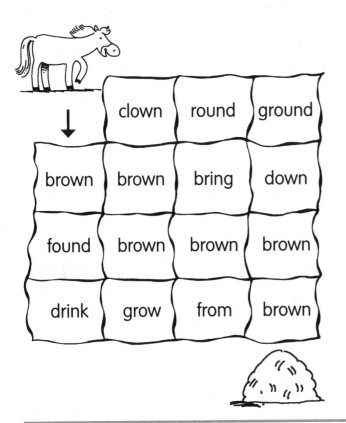

clown	round	ground
brown	brown	bring	down
found	brown	brown	brown
drink	grow	from	brown

Read. Circle each **brown**.

Hello, brown cow.

Hello, brown hen.

Hello, brown horse.

Hello, my friends.

Write **brown** to complete each sentence.

A _____ acorn fell from the tree.

I wore my _____ shoes today.

Name: _____   Date: _____

Write **brown**.

_____

- -

_____

Draw a line from each frog to the lily pad that has **brown**.

   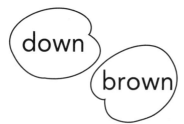

down
brown

bring
brown

   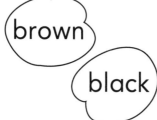

brown
black

Write the missing letters to spell **brown**.

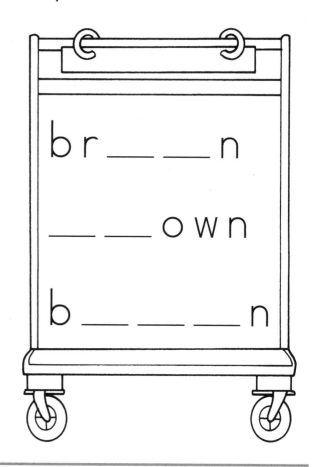

b r ___ ___ n

___ ___ o w n

b ___ ___ ___ n

Color the boxes with the letters that spell **brown**. Use brown.

b	v	a	m	y
d	r	o	k	n
p	w	e	w	h

q	x	a	w	h
p	v	o	y	n
b	r	u	x	m

Name: _____ Date: _____

Trace **eat** two times. Use red, then blue.

eat

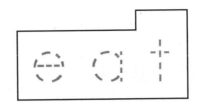

Color each space that has **eat**.
Use red.

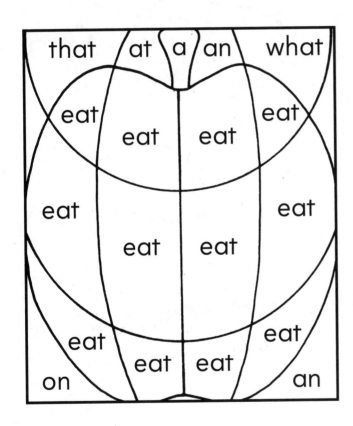

that · at · a · an · what
eat
eat · eat
eat
eat
eat
eat · eat
eat
eat
eat · eat
on · an

Read. Circle each **eat**.

I like to eat apples.

I like to eat plums.

I like to eat berries.

Oh, please get me some!

Write **eat** to complete each sentence.

A rabbit likes to _____ carrots.

Let's _____ pizza for lunch.

Name: _____ Date: _____

eat

Write **eat**.

_____

- -

_____

Help the mouse get to the cheese. Trace the path that has **eat**.

Write the missing letters to spell **eat**.

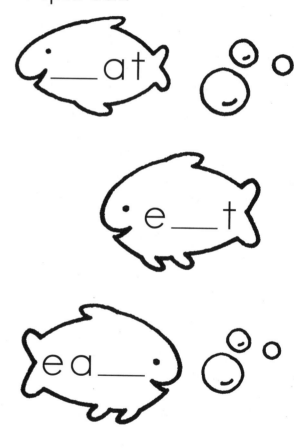

Color each set of leaves with the letters that spell **eat**. Use green.

Name: _____ Date: _____

who

Trace **who** two times. Use red, then blue.

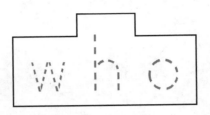

Color each space that has **who**.
Use brown.

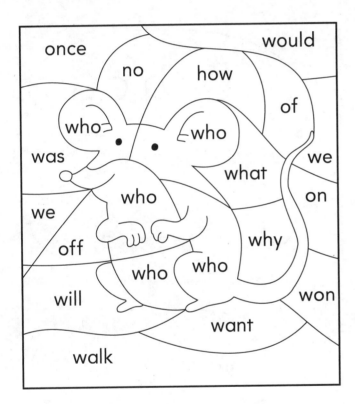

Read. Circle each **who**.

I know who is small.

I know who can squeak.

I know who has a long tail

and who wants cheese to eat!

Write **who** to complete each sentence.

Do you know _____ brought the gift?

Tell me _____ fed the dog.

Name: _____ Date: _____

who

Write **who**.

_____

_ _ _ _ _ _ _ _ _ _ _ _ _ _ _ _ _ _

_____

Help the train get to the track. Trace the path that has **who**.

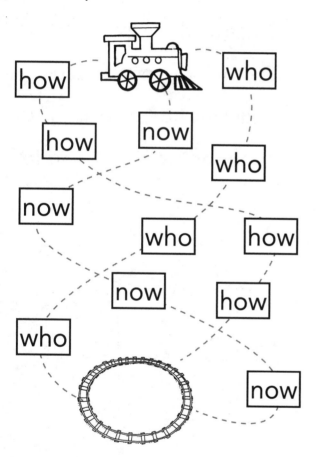

how

how   now

now   who

who   how

now   how

who

now

Write the missing letters to spell **who**.

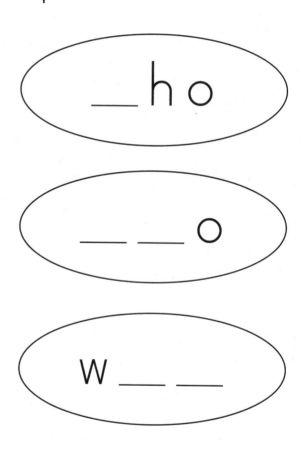

_ h o

_ _ _ o

W _ _ _

Color each part of the snake that has **who**. Use green.

how   who   who   now   who   who   won

Name: _____ Date: _____

Trace **new** two times. Use red, then blue.

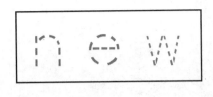

Color each pencil that has **new**.
Use yellow.

Read. Circle each **new**.

This new pencil is yellow.

This new pencil is blue.

This new pencil is red.

All of my pencils are new!

Write **new** to complete each sentence.

I have a _____ bike!

The man wore a _____ coat.

Name: _____   Date: _____

Write **new**.

_____

- - - - - - - - - - - - - - - - -

_____

Find each fox that has **new**.
Trace its path to the woods.

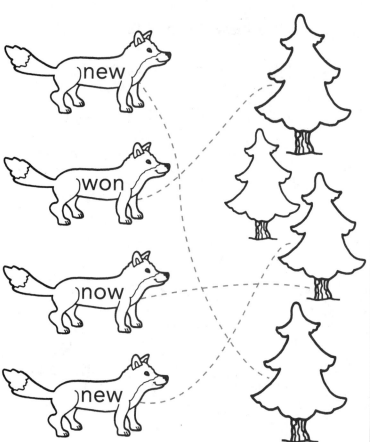

Write the missing letters
to spell **new**.

O __ e w

O n __ w

O n __ __ __

Circle each **new**.
Find the word five times.

v n a n e w
n e w n m o
u w n e w r
m r o w a v

Name: _____   Date: _____

Trace **must** two times. Use red, then blue.

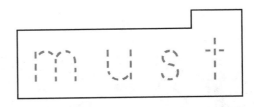

Color each snowflake that has **must**. Use blue.

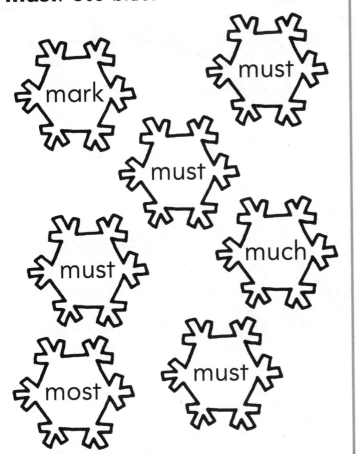

Read. Circle each **must**.

You must wear your hat.

You must wear your coat.

You must wear your boots

when you play in the snow.

Write **must** to complete each sentence.

She _____ be sad.

That man _____ have been tired.

Name: _____   Date: _____

Write **must**.

_____

- - - - - - - - - - - - - - - - -

_____

Help the cat get to the mouse.
Trace the path that has **must**.

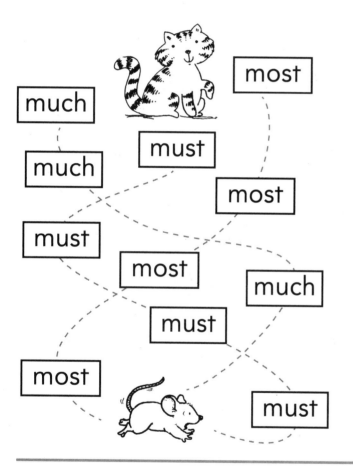

much

much

must

most

must

most

most

much

must

must

Write the missing letters
to spell **must**.

__ __ s t

m u __ __

m __ __ t

Color each pair of cupcakes with the letters that spell **must**. Use red.

mu st

mo st

mu ch

mu st

Name: _____   Date: _____

Trace **black** two times. Use red, then blue.

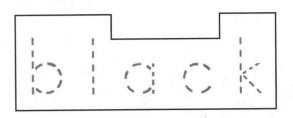

black

Color each space that has **black**.
Use black.

block

dock

but

black

black

black

black

by

be

black

black

Read. Circle each **black**.

This little car is black.

And its four wheels

are black.

It rides along a

black track.

It goes around

and comes back!

Write **black** to complete each sentence.

The sky is _____ at night.

She has _____ hair.

Name: _____ Date: _____

Write **black**.

_____

- - - - - - - - - - - - - - - - -

_____

Circle each **black**.
Find the word five times.

x f i b p h u
t u b l a c k
g b h a d e q
b l a c k p d
q a x k i h g
t c e d f o t
d k b l a c k

Color each balloon that has
black. Draw a string from
that balloon to the fence.

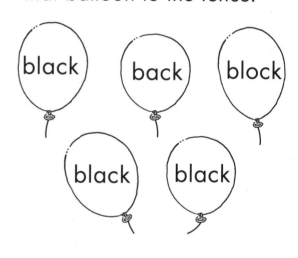

Help the chick get to the hen.
Trace the path with **black**.

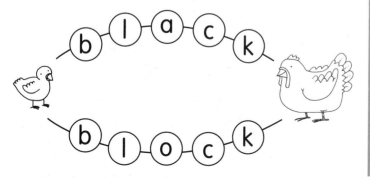

Write the missing letters
to spell **black**.

b l __ __ k

__ l a __ __

Name: _____ Date: _____

white

Trace **white** two times. Use red, then blue.

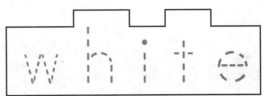

w h i t e

Help the penguin get to the iceberg. Color each space that has **white**. Use blue.

that	white	white	
work	white	why	what
when	white	that	went
walk	white	why	while
	white	when	with

Read. Circle each **white**.

What slides down white hills and plays in white snow? What walks on white ice? Why, penguins do so!

Write **white** to complete each sentence.

I have a new, _____ cap.

Large _____ snowflakes fell.

Name: _____ Date: _____

white

Write **white**.

_____

- - - - - - - - - - - - - - - - - -

_____

Find each boat that has **white**. Trace the path from that boat to the dock.

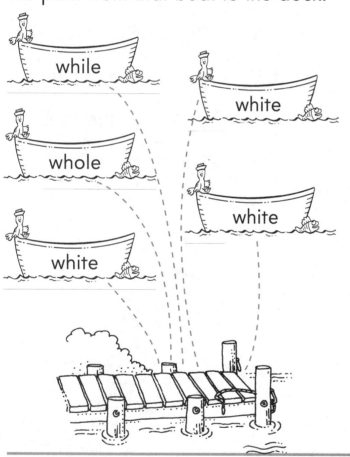

Write the missing letters to spell **white**.

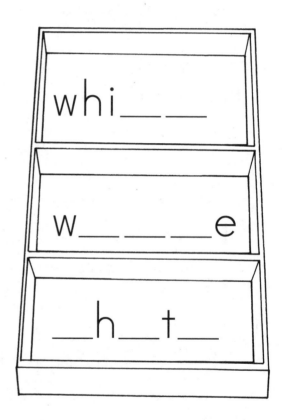

whi____

w____e

_h_t_

Color the boxes with the letters that spell **white**. Use orange.

v	d	j	k	o
m	b	i	f	e
w	h	l	t	a

w	b	j	k	e
m	h	l	t	c
r	d	i	f	a

Name: _____ Date: _____

Trace **soon** two times. Use red, then blue.

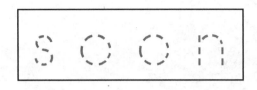

Color each planet that has **soon**. Use orange.

Read. Circle each **soon**.

I will soon be in space.

I will soon pass the sun.

I will soon see the planets.

Space travel is fun!

Write **soon** to complete each sentence.

School will start _____.

I have to go to bed _____.

Name: _____   Date: _____

Write **soon**.

_____

- - - - - - - - - - - - - - - - - -

_____

Help each cat get to its yarn.
Trace the path with **soon**.

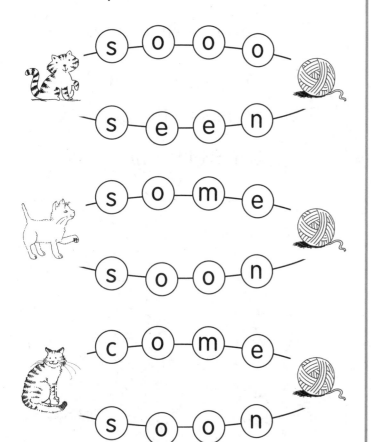

Write the missing letters
to spell **soon**.

__ O O __

s __ __ n

__ __ __ __ n

Color each pair of peas with the letters that spell **soon**. Use green.

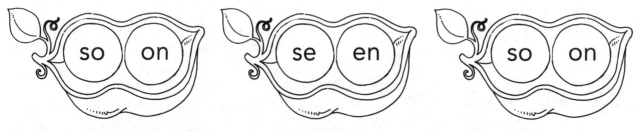

so on   se en   so on

Trace **our** two times. Use red, then blue.

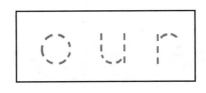

Help the kid get to the table.
Color each space that has **our**.
Use yellow.

one	our ←
won	our	our
an	your	our
or	our	our
now	our	own
	our	are

Read. Circle each **our**.

Come to our home.

Take a seat in our chair.

Have some of our meal.

We are happy to share!

Write **our** to complete each sentence.

This is _____ rake.

Dad took _____ junk away.

Name: _____ Date: _____

our

Write **our**.

_____

- - - - - - - - - - - - - - - - - -

_____

Circle each **our**.
Find the word five times.

p	c	o	v
e	n	u	m
o	u	r	o
c	m	e	u
v	o	n	r
o	u	r	a
p	r	g	e

Write the missing letters
to spell **our**.

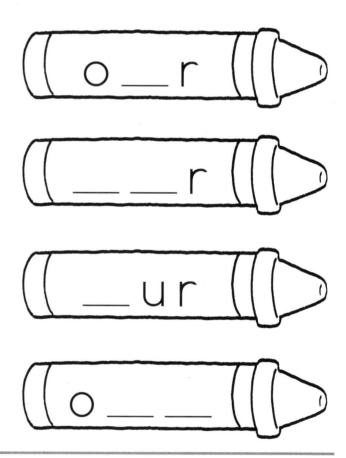

o _ r

_ _ r

_ u r

o _ _ _

Color each flower with the letters that spell **our**. Use yellow.

o u r   a r e   o u r   o n e

Name: _____   Date: _____

Trace **ate** two times. Use red, then blue.

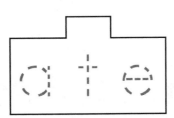

Color each space that has **ate**.
Use red.

Read. Circle each **ate**.

My dog ate its bone.

My bird ate its seed.

My fish ate its food.

They ate all that they need!

Write **ate** to complete each sentence.

I _____ grapes at lunch.

The squirrel _____ an acorn.

Name: _____   Date: _____

Write **ate**.

_____

- -

_____

Find each leaf that has **ate**. Trace the path from that leaf to the basket.

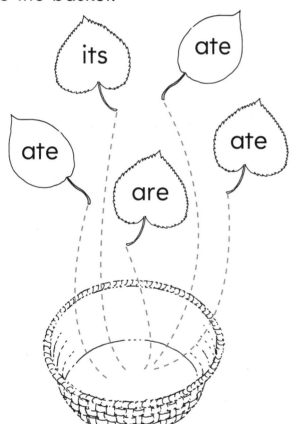

Write the missing letters to spell **ate**.

Color the two socks with the letters that spell **ate**. Use orange.

Name: _____ Date: _____

Trace **say** two times. Use red, then blue.

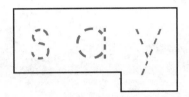

Color each space that has **say**.
Use yellow.

Read. Circle each **say**.

What do you say

when you're happy?

What do you say

when you're sad?

What do you say

when you're scared?

What do you say

when you're mad?

Write **say** to complete each sentence.

Can you _____ the answer?

I like to _____ the alphabet. **ABC**

Name: _____   Date: _____

Write **say**.

_____

- -

_____

Connect the dots to spell **say**.
Find the word two times.

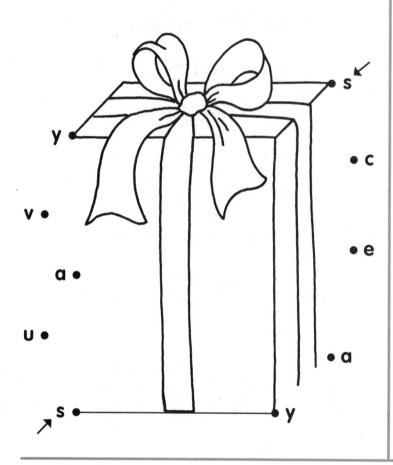

Write the missing letters
to spell **say**.

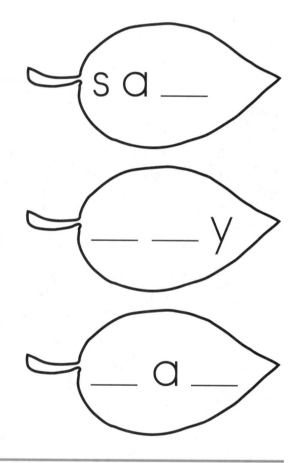

s a ___

___ ___ ___ y

___ a ___

Color each acorn that has **say**. Use brown.

 say
 any
 say
 say
 yes

Name: _____   Date: _____

Trace **under** two times. Use red, then blue.

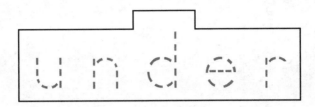

Help the car get to the country.
Color each space that has **under**.
Use gray.

	under	under	until
and	over	under	upon
under	under	under	put
under	then	unless	run
under	under	under	

Read. Circle each **under**.

We ride under the big sky.

We ride under the trees.

We ride under the bright sun

on our ride into the country.

Write **under** to complete each sentence.

The dog is _____ the stool.

Roots grow _____ the ground.

Name: _____   Date: _____

Write **under**.

_____

- -

_____

Color each kite that has **under**. Draw a string from that kite to the kangaroo.

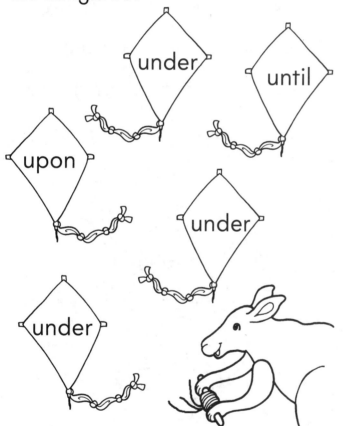

Write the missing letters to spell **under**.

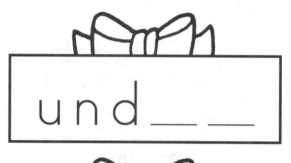

u n d ___ ___ ___

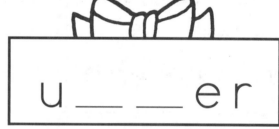

u ___ ___ ___ e r

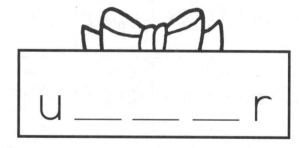

u ___ ___ ___ ___ r

Color each pair of apples with the letters that spell **under**. Use red.

Name: _____   Date: _____

Trace **please** two times. Use red, then blue.

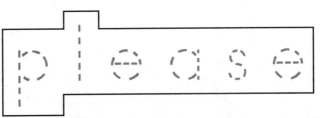

Color each pea that has **please**. Use green.

Read. Circle each **please**.

Wash your face, please.

Brush your teeth, please.

Eat your peas, please.

Mom asks me to do

all of these.

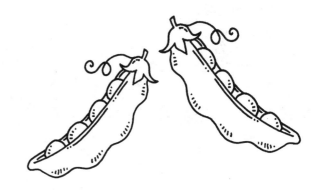

Write **please** to complete each sentence.

Can I read your book, _____?

I would like a drink, _____.

Name: _____   Date: _____

Write **please**.

_____

- - - - - - - - - - - - - - - - - -

_____

Find each spaceship that has **please**. Draw a line from that spaceship to the alien.

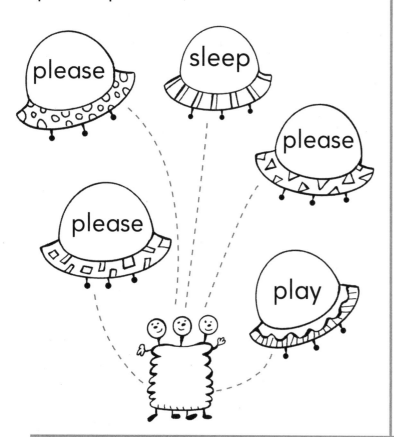

Write the missing letters to spell **please**.

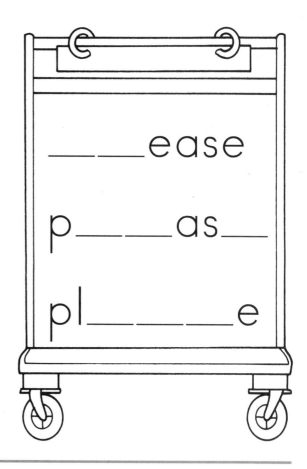

____ease

p____as____

pl_____e

Color each pair of cupcakes with the letters that spell **please**. Use blue.

Name: _____   Date: _____

Trace **of** two times. Use red, then blue.

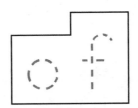

Color each space that has **of**.
Use pink.

Read. Circle each **of**.

I put in all of my pennies.

I put in all of my dimes.

I put in all of my nickels and

my quarters all of the time.

Write **of** to complete each sentence.

The birds ate all _____ the seeds.

The man got off _____ his horse.

Name: _____   Date: _____

of

Write **of** two times.

_____   _____

_____   _____

_____   _____

Draw a line from each duck to the puddle that has **of**.

   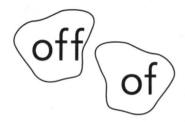

off   of

   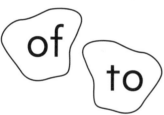

of   to

   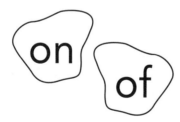

on   of

Write **of** on each duck.

Color each owl that has **of**. Use gray.

of   of   of   off   to   of   of   if

Name: _____ Date: _____

 his

Trace **his** two times. Use red, then blue.

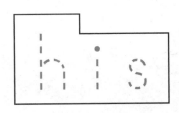

Color each ribbon that has **his**.
Use blue.

him | this | his

his | hit

has | his | his

Read. Circle each **his**.

The prince wore

his blue ribbon.

He wore his

red ribbon, too.

Then he got out

all of his ribbons

to show to me

and you.

Write **his** to complete each sentence.

The boy waved _____ hand.

The king is wearing _____ crown.

Name: _____ Date: _____

| his |

Write **his**.

_____
- -
_____

Circle each **his**.
Find the word five times.

b e c j
f h i s
h u d h
i c k i
s j h s
e d i f
h i s k

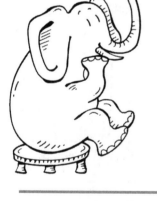

Write the missing letters
to spell **his**.

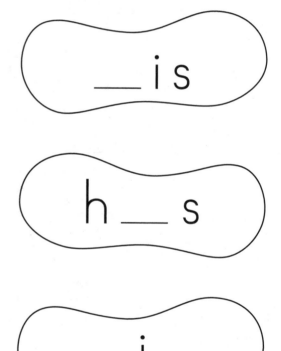

__ i s

h __ s

__ i __

Help the car get to the Finish line. Trace the path that has **his**.

his — his
          his   has — has   FINISH
has — has   his — his

Name: _____ Date: _____

Trace **had** two times. Use red, then blue.

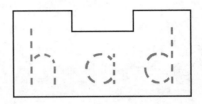

Color each space that has **had**.
Use brown.

Read. Circle each **had**.

I had a little teddy bear

that had a big bow tie.

One day I had to

wash my bear.

I really don't know why.

Write **had** to complete each sentence.

I _____ to wipe up the spill.

The girl _____ fun on the swing.

Name: _____ Date: _____

Write **had**.

_____

- - - - - - - - - - - - - - - - - - - -

_____

Draw a line from each frog to the lily pad that has **had**.

 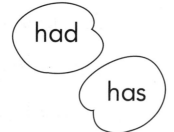
had
has

 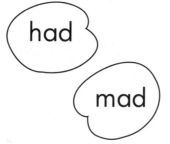
had
mad

 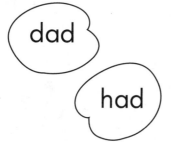
dad
had

Write the missing letters to spell **had**.

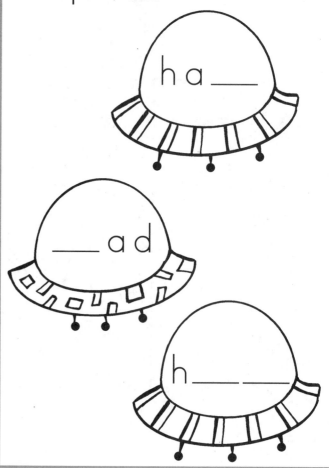
h a ___
___ a d
h ___

Color each computer that has **had**. Use green.

dad   had   has   had   had

Name: _____ Date: _____

Trace **him** two times. Use red, then blue.

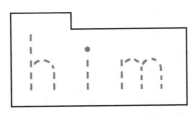

Color each gift that has **him**.
Use red.

 him
 his
 him

 fun
 him
 had

 am
 hid
 him

 then
 him
 her

Read. Circle each **him**.

On Bob's birthday,

we gave him a party.

We gave him gifts and

played games with him, too.

Then we gave him a

birthday cake and sang,

"Happy Birthday to You!"

Write **him** to complete each sentence.

Tim wants me to watch _____ flip.

We gave _____ some logs to cut.

Name: _____   Date: _____

Write **him**.

_____

_____

Find each acorn that has **him**.
Trace the path from that acorn
to the squirrel.

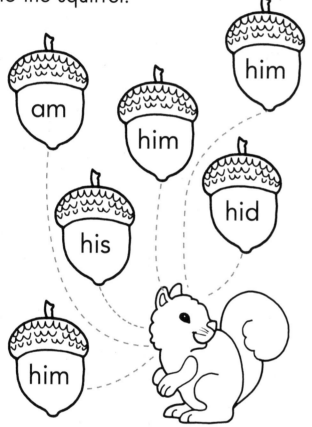

Write the missing letters
to spell **him**.

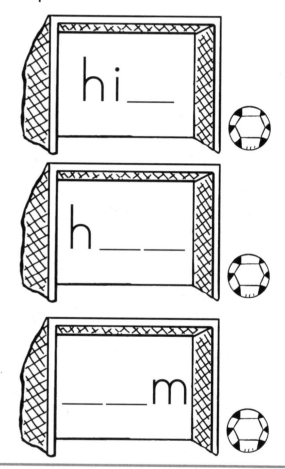

Color the two shoes with the letters that spell **him**. Use orange.

Name: _____   Date: _____

Trace **her** two times. Use red, then blue.

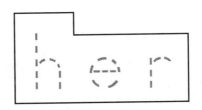

Color each cupcake that has **her**. Use yellow.

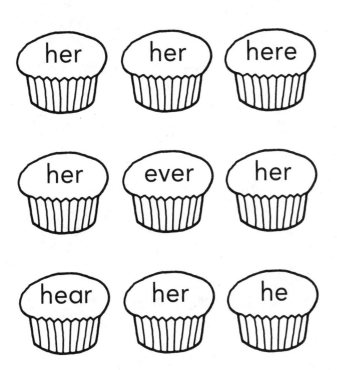

Read. Circle each **her**.

We like to eat her cupcakes.

We like to eat her pies.

We like to eat her cookies.

She makes the best, oh my!

Write **her** to complete each sentence.

The girl read _____ book in a chair.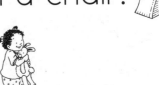

She hugged _____ bunny.

Name: _____ Date: _____

her

Write **her**.

_____

- - - - - - - - - - - - - -

_____

Circle each **her**.
Find the word five times.

b h a v

w e h u

o r e b

h e r h

d a v e

u h e r

Write the missing letters
to spell **her**.

he___

h_____

_____r

Color the set of friends with the letters that spell **her**. Use blue.

Name: _____ Date: _____

Trace **some** two times. Use red, then blue.

Color each heart that has **some**.
Use red.

Read. Circle each **some**.

Let's cut out some circles.

Let's cut out some hearts.

Let's cut out some squares.

Let's do some art!

Write **some** to complete each sentence.

Can I have _____ gum?

The boy drank _____ water.

Name: _____ Date: _____

Write **some**.

_____

- -

_____

Connect the dots to spell **some**.
Find the word two times.

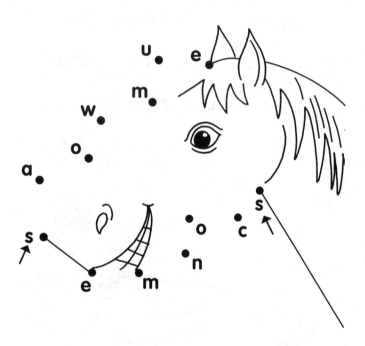

Write the missing letters
to spell **some**.

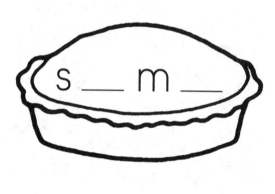

s __ m __

__ o __ e

Color the glasses that have **some** on both sides. Use blue.

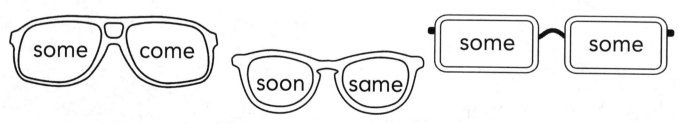

some / come   soon / same   some   some

Name: _____ Date: _____

as

Trace **as** two times. Use red, then blue.

Help the clown get to the circus.
Color each space that has **as**.
Use orange.

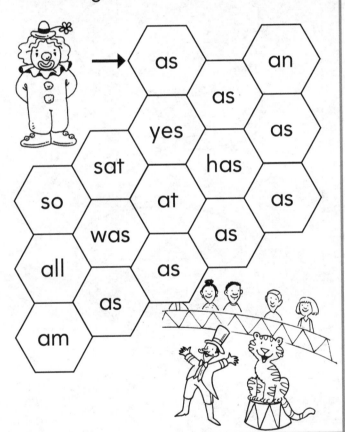

Read. Circle each **as**.

I'm as quiet as a mouse.

I'm as tall as a giraffe.

I'm as funny as a clown.

I can make you laugh!

Write **as** to complete each sentence.

We walked _____ slow _____ a snail.

He counted _____ he hopped.

Name: _____   Date: _____

as

Write **as** two times.

_____   _____

_____   _____

_____   _____

Find each fish that has **as**.
Trace its path to the water.

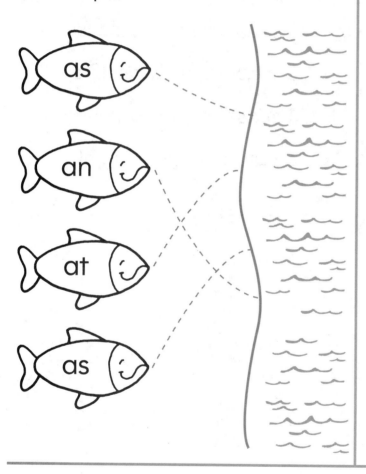

as

an

at

as

Write **as** on each yo-yo.

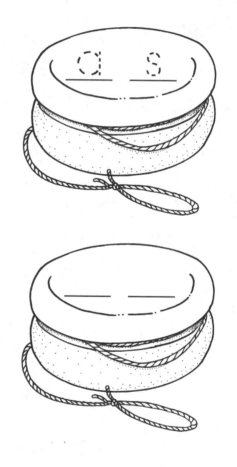

Color each train car that has **as**. Use purple.

as | is | as | am | as

Name: _____ Date: _____

then

Trace **then** two times. Use red, then blue.

Color each book that has **then**.
Use orange.

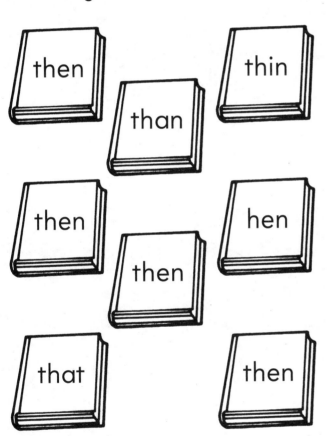

then | than | thin
then | then | hen
that | | then

Read. Circle each **then**.

I will read, then go eat.

I will read, then go play.

I will read, then go sleep.

But then, I might just

read all day!

Write **then** to complete each sentence.

Eat your carrots, _____ your pie.

Put on your socks, _____ your shoes. 👟

Name: _____ Date: _____

Write **then**.

_____

- -

_____

Help each raindrop get to the ground. Connect the dots to spell **then**. Start at **t**.

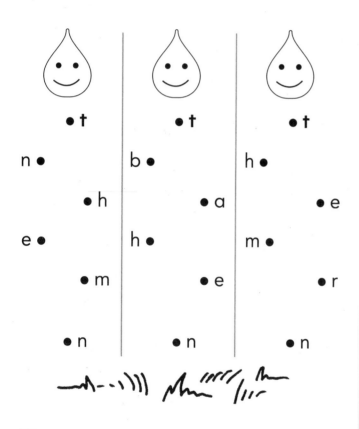

Write the missing letters to spell **then**.

t __ e __

t h __ __ __

__ __ e n

Color each bat with the letters that spell **then**. Use brown.

Name: _____   Date: _____

Trace **could** two times. Use red, then blue.

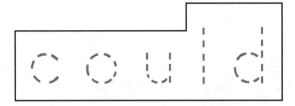

Help the kid get down the hill.
Color each space that has **could**.
Use gray.

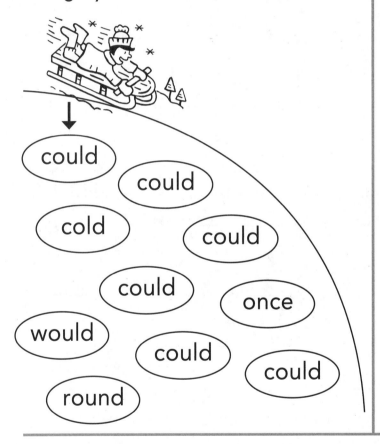

could
could
cold
could
could
would
once
could
could
round

Read. Circle each **could**.

I wish I could skate.

I wish I could ski.

I wish I could sled

down a snowy hill—

whee!

Write **could** to complete each sentence.

The band _____ play well.

We _____ hear the boy yell.

Name: _____ Date: _____

could

Write **could**.

_____

_____

_____

Circle each **could**.
Find the word five times.

e	b	t	v	a	c
c	o	u	l	d	o
o	p	f	c	w	u
u	v	q	o	p	l
l	c	o	u	l	d
d	f	p	l	e	t
b	a	g	d	f	q

Write the missing letters
to spell **could**.

c o u __ __ __

__ __ __ u l d

c __ __ __ __ d

Color each robot that has **could**. Use purple.

would

could

could

cold

Name: _____ Date: _____

when

Trace **when** two times. Use red, then blue.

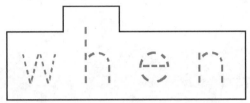

Help the frog get to the rock. Color each lily pad with **when**. Use green.

when

when

when

when

were

who

when

hen

where

when

Read. Circle each **when**.

I see you when you sit.

I see you when you swim.

I see you when you jump

up high to catch

a big, black fly.

Write **when** to complete each sentence.

Call me _____ you get home.

I know _____ school starts.

Name: _____ Date: _____

 when

Write **when**.

_____

- - - - - - - - - - - - - - - - - - -

_____

Connect the dots to spell **when**.
Find the word two times.

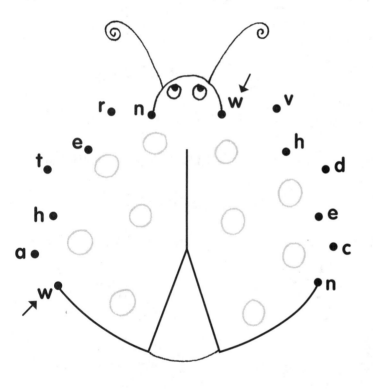

Write the missing letters
to spell **when**.

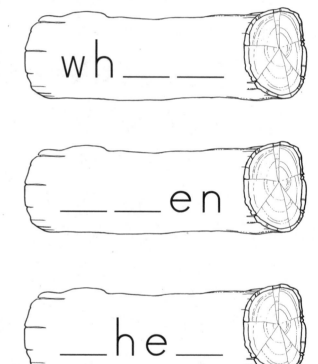

wh____

____en

__he__

Color each turtle that has **when**. Use green.

where   when   when   what

Name: _____ Date: _____

were

Trace **were** two times. Use red, then blue.

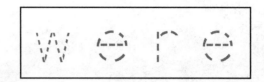

w e r e

Color each space that has **were**. Use purple.

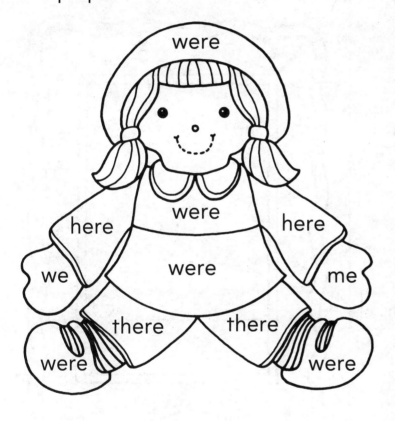

were

here   were   here

we   were   me

there   there

were   were

Read. Circle each **were**.

There were bears

and balls.

There were bats

and blocks.

There were tops

and dolls

in my little toy box.

Write **were** to complete each sentence.

The leaves _____ falling.

What page _____ you on?

Name: _____   Date: _____

were

Write **were**.

_____

- - - - - - - - - - - - - - - - - - - -

_____

Help the pig get to its ribbon.
Trace the path that has **were**.

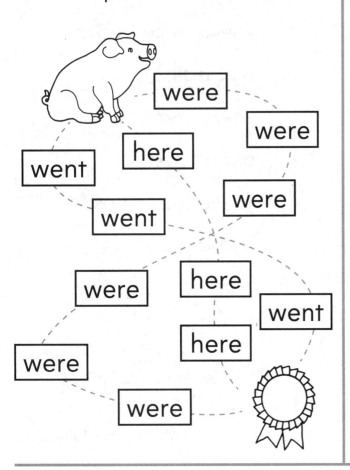

Write the missing letters
to spell **were**.

W___ ___ e

___ e r ___

___ ___ ___ e

Color each pair of clouds with the letters that spell **were**. Use blue.

Name: _____   Date: _____

them

Trace **them** two times. Use red, then blue.

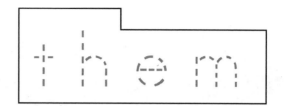

Color each space that has **them**.
Use orange.

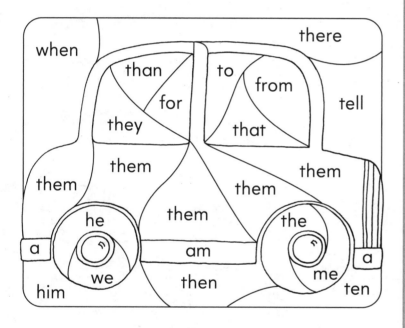

Read. Circle each **them**.

People ride in this.
It takes them
all around.
It takes them
to the country,
and it takes them
into town.
What is it?
A car!

Write **them** to complete each sentence.

Look at _____ run!

Take the sticks and play _____.

Name: _____ Date: _____

 them

Write **them**.

_____

- -

_____

Connect the dots to spell **them**.
Find the word two times.

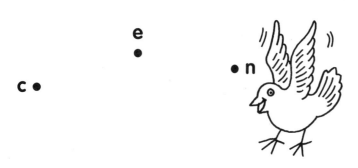
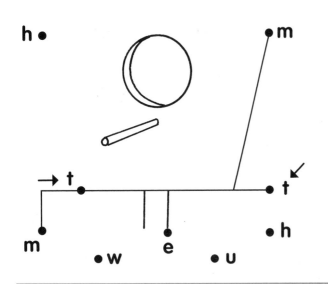

Write the missing letters
to spell **them**.

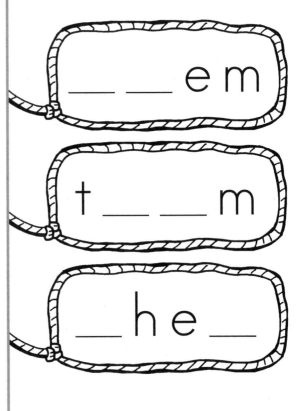

____ e m

t ____ m

__ h e __

Color each pair of cows with the letters that spell **them**. Use red.

th em   th ey   th en   th em

Name: _____   Date: _____

 **ask**

Trace **ask** two times. Use red, then blue.

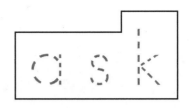

Help the diver get to the chest. Color each space that has **ask**. Use blue.

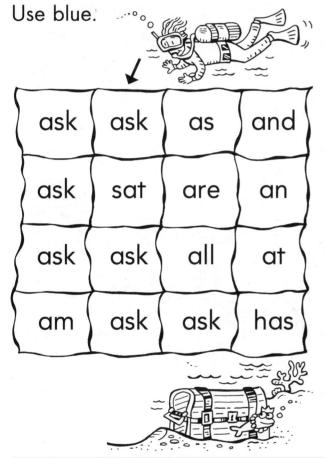

ask	ask	as	and
ask	sat	are	an
ask	ask	all	at
am	ask	ask	has

Read. Circle each **ask**.

Let's ask the diver

where she went.

Let's ask her

what she found.

Let's ask her when she

takes a swim,

if fish are all around.

Write **ask** to complete each sentence.

I will _____ Dad to help me ride.

Please _____ the boy to sweep.

Name: _____ Date: _____

 **ask**

Write **ask**.

_____

_____

_____

Help the mouse get to the cheese. Trace the path that has **ask**.

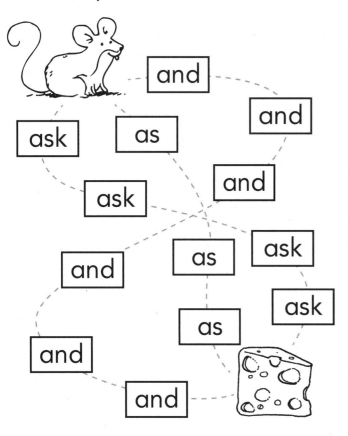

Write the missing letters to spell **ask**.

__ sk

a __ __ k

as __

Circle each **ask**. Find the word five times.

f a s k n t
a s k c e a
e k u n t s
x a s k u k

The Jumbo Book of Sight Word Practice Pages © 2013 by Immacula A. Rhodes, Scholastic Teaching Resources • page 242

Name: _____ Date: _____

Trace **an** two times. Use red, then blue.

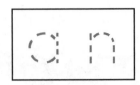

Help the ant get to the apple.
Color each grass patch that has
an. Use green.

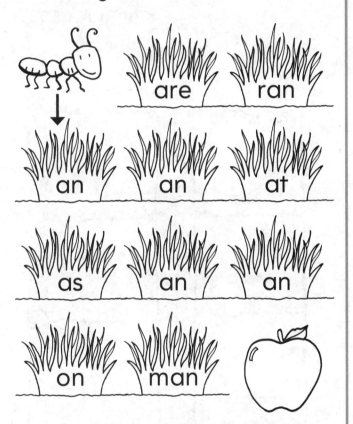

Read. Circle each **an**.

Once I saw an ant

eat an apple and an egg.

Then I saw that ant

go up an elephant's leg!

Write **an** to complete each sentence.

I want to be _____ astronaut.

There was _____ insect in my cup.

Name: _____ Date: _____

Write **an** two times.

_____ _____

_____ _____

_____ _____

Color each pair of jellybeans with the letters that spell **an**. Use red.

Write **an** on each block.

Color each part of the snake that has **an**. Use orange.

in | an | an | as | an | an | and

Name: _____   Date: _____

Trace **over** two times. Use red, then blue.

Help Bear get to the tree. Color each space that has **over**. Use brown.

Read. Circle each **over**.

The bear went

over the mountain.

The bear went

over the mountain.

The bear went

over the mountain

to get to the honey!

Write **over** to complete each sentence.

A balloon went _____ the house.

Put the flower _____ there.

Name: _____ Date: _____

Write **over**.

_____
- -
_____

Find each frog that has **over**.
Trace its path to the water.

Write the missing letters
to spell **over**.

_____ er

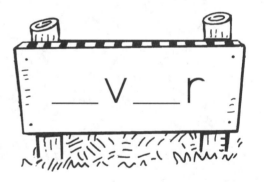

__ v __ r

Color each pair of trees with the letters that spell **over**. Use green.

Name: _____   Date: _____

just

Trace **just** two times. Use red, then blue.

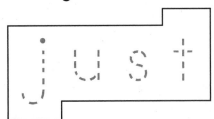

Color each flower that has **just**. Use pink.

Read. Circle each **just**.

I just met a unicorn

with just one nose

and mouth and tail.

And on its head

was just one horn.

We just made friends—

I think that's swell!

Write **just** to complete each sentence.

It _____ started to rain.

I want _____ one grape.

Name: _____   Date: _____

just

Write **just**.

_____

_____

_____

Find each boat that has **just**. Trace the path from that boat to the dock.

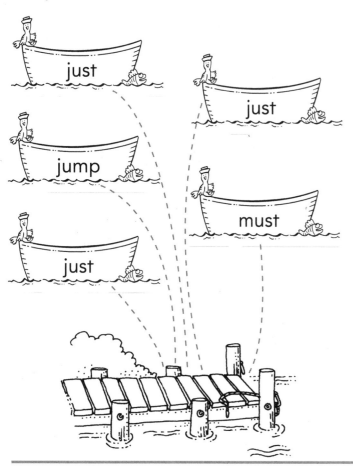

just

just

jump

must

just

Write the missing letters to spell **just**.

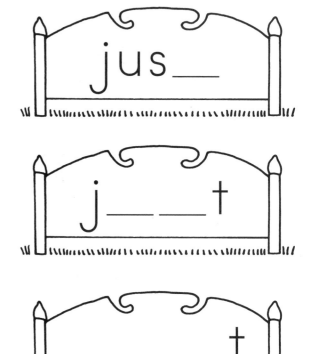

j u s ___

j ___ ___ ___ t

___ ___ ___ ___ t

Color each flower with the letters that spell **just**. Use yellow.

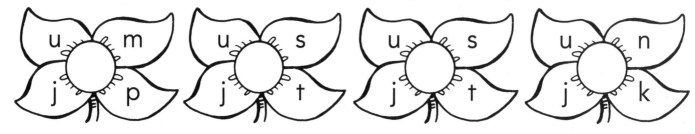

Name: _____ Date: _____

from

Trace **from** two times. Use red, then blue.

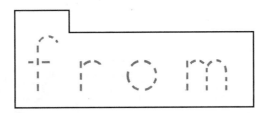

Color each space that has **from**. Use green.

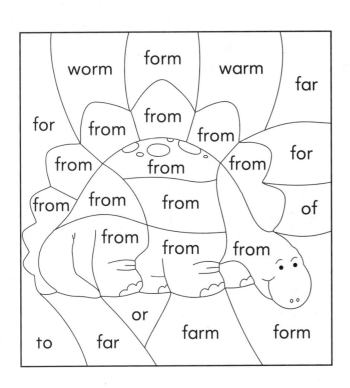

Read. Circle each **from**.

We hear about dinosaurs

from long, long ago.

But where did they come from?

Do you know?

They came from eggs!

Write **from** to complete each sentence.

She just came _____ the store.

Pick peas _____ the garden.

Name: _____   Date: _____

from

Write **from**.

_____

- - - - - - - - - - - - - - - - - - - -

_____

Circle each **from**.
Find the word five times.

m t a f v u
v n k r e f
u f r o m r
f r o m x o
n e f r o m

Write the missing letters
to spell **from**.

_ r _ m

f _ _ m

f r _ _ _

Color each fish bowl that has **from**. Use blue.

 from  front  for  from  form

Name: _____ Date: _____

Trace **any** two times. Use red, then blue.

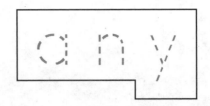

Color each jellybean that has **any**. Use purple.

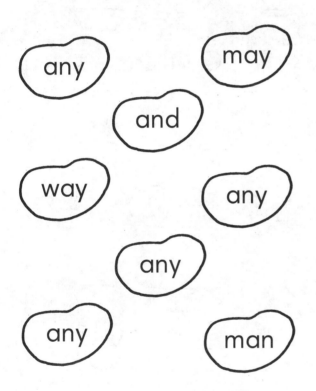

Read. Circle each **any**.

Do you want any jellybeans?

Do you want any candy?

You can have any kind.

See, I have plenty!

Write **any** to complete each sentence.

I don't have _____ crayons.

Take _____ book you want.

Name: _____ Date: _____

Write **any**.

_____

- -

_____

Find each rabbit that has **any**.
Trace its path to the woods.

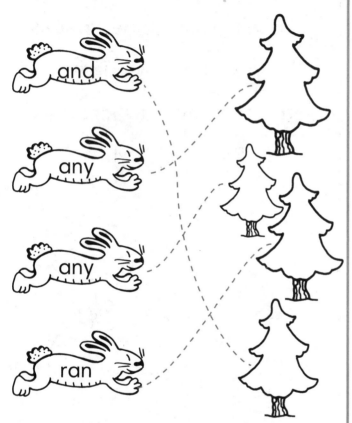

Write the missing letters
to spell **any**.

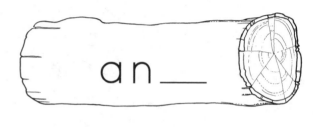

a n __

__ n y

__ __ y

Color each stack of blocks with the letters that spell **any**. Use red.

Name: _____   Date: _____

Trace **how** two times. Use red, then blue.

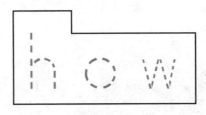

Color each pie that has **how**.
Use brown.

how	show
now	how
know	how
how	low

Read. Circle each **how**.

Just how long does it take

to make three apple pies?

And how long does it take

to bake those yummy pies?

Write **how** to complete each sentence.

Do you know _____ to knit?

Just _____ did this mess get here?

Name: _____   Date: _____

how

Write **how**.

_____

- - - - - - - - - - - - - - - - - - - -

_____

Circle each **how**.
Find the word five times.

h	o	w	v
o	d	h	e
w	n	o	h
m	h	w	o
v	o	b	w
u	w	a	m

Write the missing letters
to spell **how**.

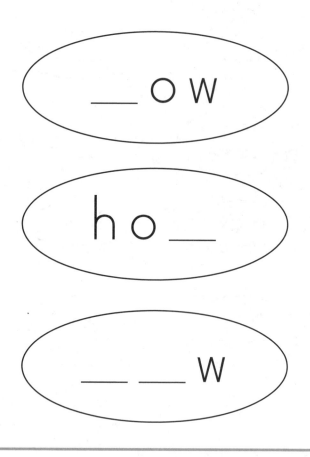

(__ o w)

(h o __)

(__ __ w)

Color each set of balls with the letters that spell **how**. Use orange.

Name: _____   Date: _____

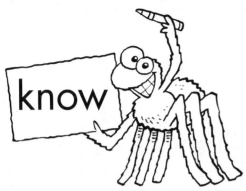

Trace **know** two times. Use red, then blue.

Color each chef hat that has **know**. Use yellow.

Read. Circle each **know**.

Do you know the Muffin Man?

Yes, I know the Muffin Man.

Do you know what's in his pan?

Yes, I know what's in his pan.

It's a tasty treat!

Write **know** to complete each sentence.

I _____ what's in the egg!

Did you _____ he won?

Name: _____   Date: _____

Write **know**.

_____

- - - - - - - - - - - - - - - -

_____

Find each ball that has **know**. Trace the path from that ball to the basket.

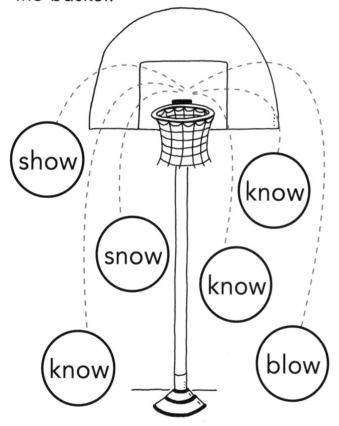

Write the missing letters to spell **know**.

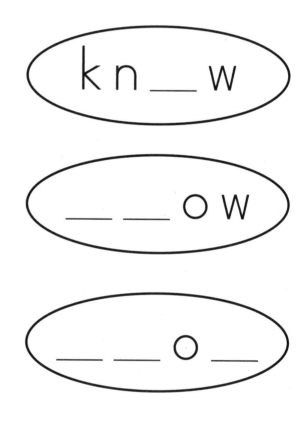

k n __ w

____ o w

____ o __

Color the two puzzle pieces with the letters that spell **know**. Use blue.

kn   ot   ow

kn   ow   it

kn   ee   ow

Name: _____   Date: _____

Trace **put** two times. Use red, then blue.

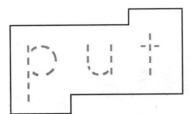

Color each toy that has **put**.
Use red.

Read. Circle each **put**.

I'll put one toy on the table.

You put one toy on the floor.

I'll put one toy in the window.

You put one by the door.

Write **put** to complete each sentence.

He _____ a log on the fire.

I _____ a funny hat on the pig.

Name: _____   Date: _____

put

Write **put**.

_____

- - - - - - - - - - - - - - - - - - -

_____

Find each snail that has **put**.
Trace its path to the grass.

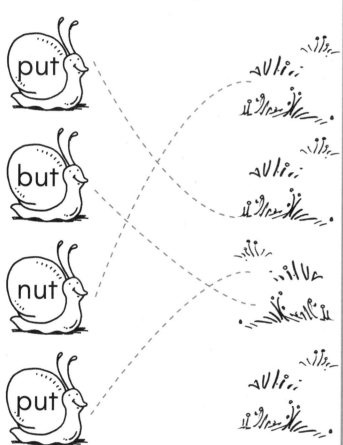

Write the missing letters
to spell **put**.

p u __

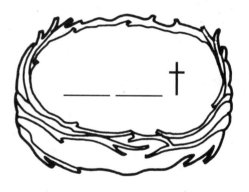

__ __ t

Color each set of leaves with the letters that spell **put**. Use green.

Name: _____ Date: _____

Trace **take** two times. Use red, then blue.

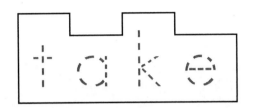

Color each space that has **take**.
Use blue.

Read. Circle each **take**.

A helicopter can take you

up and down.

It can take you all around.

It can take you

from side to side.

Let's go take

a helicopter ride!

Write **take** to complete each sentence.

We _____ turns to play.

Let's _____ a trip to the moon!

Name: _____   Date: _____

Write **take**.

_____

- -

_____

Connect the dots to spell **take**.
Find the word two times.

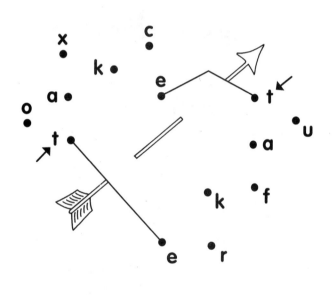

Write the missing letters to spell **take**.

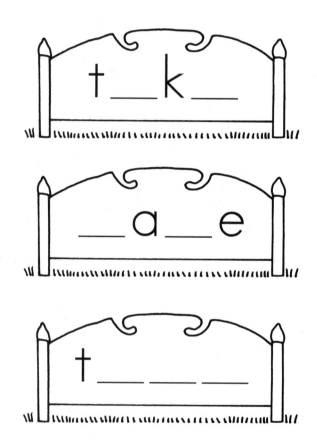

t __ k __

__ a __ e

t __ __ __

Color each yo-yo that has **take**. Use orange.

take   late   take   take   make

The Jumbo Book of Sight Word Practice Pages © 2013 by Immacula A. Rhodes, Scholastic Teaching Resources • page 260

Name: _____ Date: _____

Trace **every** two times. Use red, then blue.

Color each space that has **every**. Use orange.

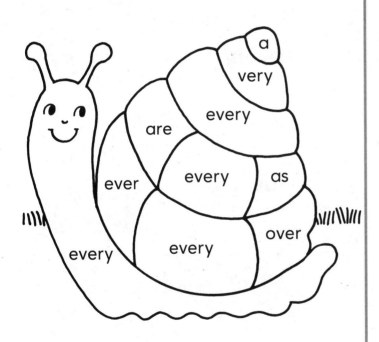

Read. Circle each **every**.

Does every snail have a shell?

Does every snail move slow?

Does every snail like to crawl?

I really want to know.

Write **every** to complete each sentence.

I did _____ puzzle in class.

We counted _____ seed.

Name: _____ Date: _____

every

Write **every**.

_____

- - - - - - - - - - - - - - - - - - -

_____

Circle each **every**.
Find the word five times.

j c e v e r y
u z q h v p o
e p a w e x k
v o n j r u g
e v e r y c i
r a g k z x n
y e v e r y w

Color each ice-cream scoop
that has **every**. Draw a line
from that scoop to a cone.

every   very
        every
ever   every

Help the spider get to the web.
Trace the path with **every**.

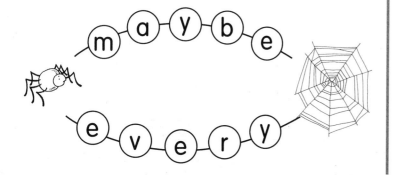

m a y b e
e v e r y

Write the missing letters
to spell **every**.

e __ __ __ y

__ v __ r __

Name: _____ Date: _____

Trace **old** two times. Use red, then blue.

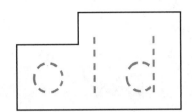

Help the lady get to her house.
Color each space that has **old**.
Use brown.

off   old   old

old   could   on

cold   old   all

once   old   long

old

old   old   odd

Read. Circle each **old**.

Once an old lady

lived in an old shoe.

Her things were all old.

She had nothing new.

Write **old** to complete each sentence.

We live in an _____ house.

She used an _____ rag.

Name: _____   Date: _____

Write **old**.

_____

_ _ _ _ _ _ _ _ _ _ _ _ _ _ _ _ _

_____

Help each bowling ball get to its pin. Connect the dots to spell **old**. Start at **o**.

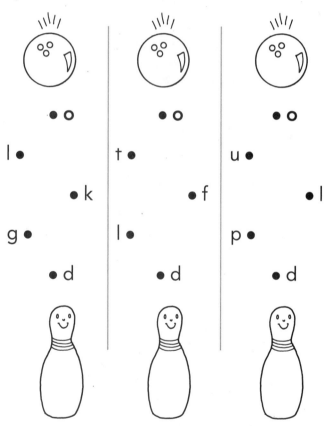

Write the missing letters to spell **old**.

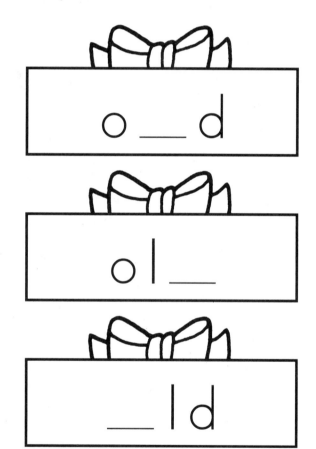

o __ d

o l __

__ l d

Color each set of candles with the letters that spell **old**. Use blue.

Name: _____ Date: _____

Trace **by** two times. Use red, then blue.

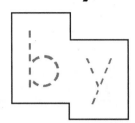

Color each space that has **by**.
Use blue.

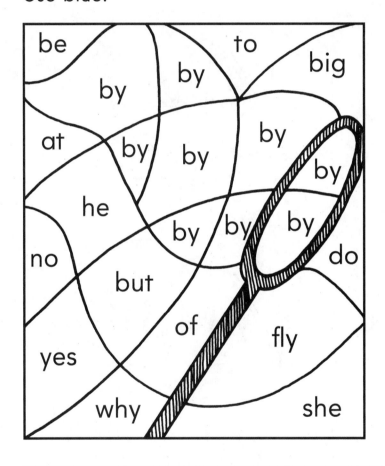

Read. Circle each **by**.

A mouse ran by.

I caught it in my net.

A frog hopped by.

I caught it in my net.

A snake slid by.

I let it go on by!

Write **by** to complete each sentence.

Our bus went _____ the school.

I found a pen _____ the bed. ✒

Name: _____ Date: _____

Write **by** two times.

_____ _____

_____ _____

_____ _____

Find each coin that has **by**. Trace the path from that coin to the bank.

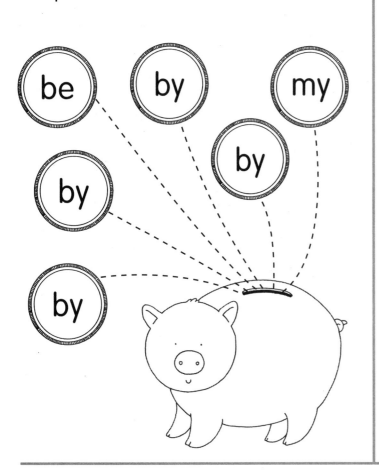

Write **by** on each tent.

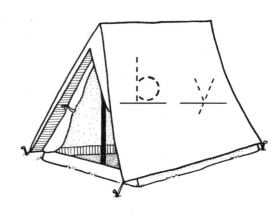

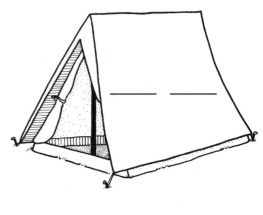

Color each pair of blocks with the letters that spell **by**. Use green.

  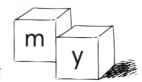 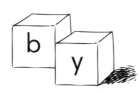 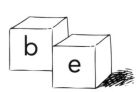

Name: _____   Date: _____

Trace **after** two times. Use red, then blue.

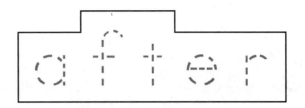

Help Bear get to the ride. Color each space that has **after**. Use red.

other	after	also
again	after	after
ask	and	after
after	after	after
after	often	onto

Read. Circle each **after**.

One day after school,

Bear went to the fair.

Bear rode the cups

after she got there.

Write **after** to complete each sentence.

Our train comes _____ this one.

Can I swing _____ you?

Name: _____ Date: _____

Write **after**.

_____

_ _ _ _ _ _ _ _ _ _ _ _ _ _ _ _ _

_____

Circle each **after**.
Find the word five times.

a f t e r a
f o u w a f
t h v n f t
e x e u t e
r a f t e r
x h o v r n

Write the missing letters
to spell **after**.

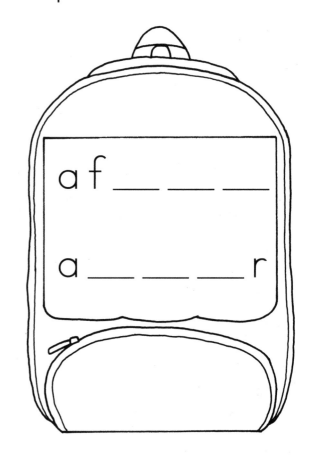

a f _ _ _ _ _

a _ _ _ _ _ r

Color each pair of cupcakes with the letters that spell **after**. Use pink.

Name: _____ Date: _____

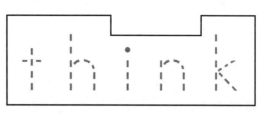

Trace **think** two times. Use red, then blue.

Color each boat that has **think**. Use red.

think   thing   thin

thank   think

this   think   think

Read. Circle each **think**.

I think I'll take

the red boat.

No, I think I'll take

the blue.

What do you think?

What would you do?

Write **think** to complete each sentence.

I like to _____ about airplanes.

I _____ the cat is hiding.

Name: _____ Date: _____

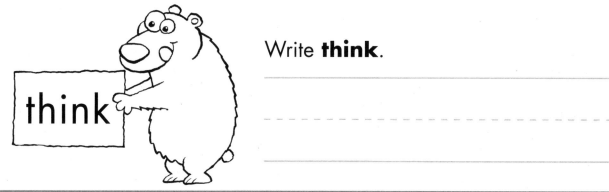

Write **think**.

_____

- - - - - - - - - - - - - - - - -

_____

Connect the dots to spell **think**.
Find the word two times.

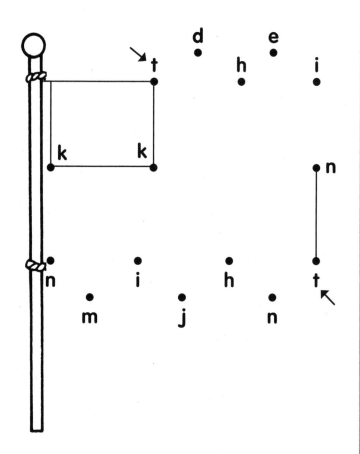

Write the missing letters
to spell **think**.

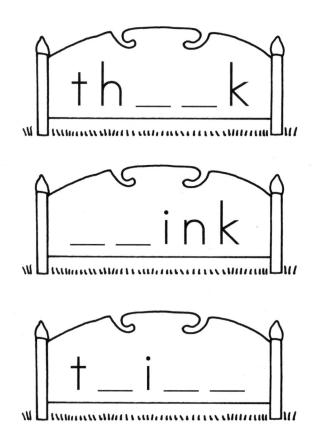

t h ___ ___ k

___ ___ i n k

t ___ i ___ ___

Color each chick that has **think**. Use yellow.

thing   thin   think   think   think

Name: _____   Date: _____

Trace **let** two times. Use red, then blue.

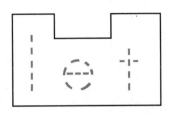

Color each space that has **let**.
Use purple.

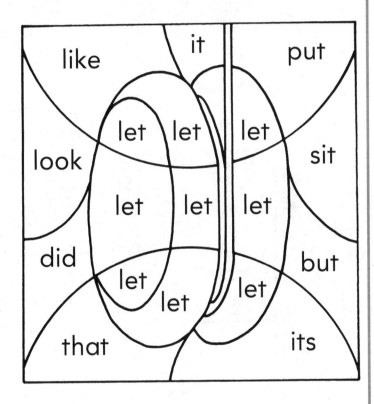

Read. Circle each **let**.

Please let me use your yo-yo.

I'll let you use my jacks.

And when you finish playing,

let me put them in my sack.

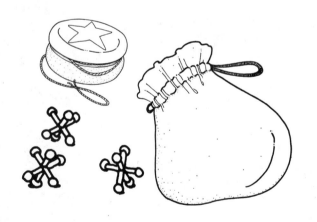

Write **let** to complete each sentence.

Dad _____ me play in the snow.

I _____ my friend slide first.

Name: _____   Date: _____

Write **let**.

_____

- - - - - - - - - - - - - - - - - - -

_____

Help each cat get to its yarn.
Trace the path with **let**.

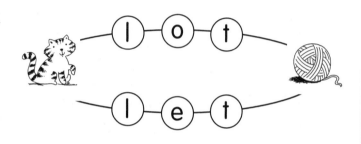

l – o – t

l – e – t

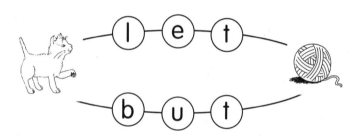

l – e – t

b – u – t

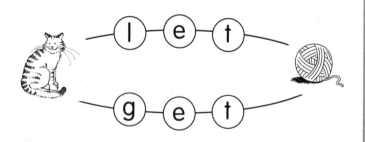

l – e – t

g – e – t

Write the missing letters
to spell **let**.

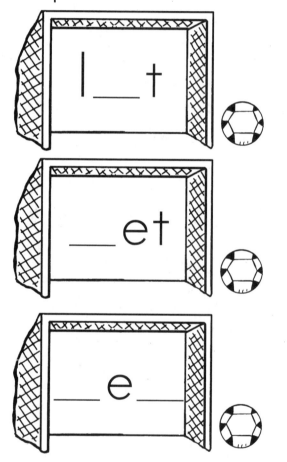

l __ t

__ e t

__ e __

Circle each **let**.
Find the word five times.

l e t l e t
e f a u l o
t l e t e f
a h c o t k

Name: _____ Date: _____

going

Trace **going** two times. Use red, then blue.

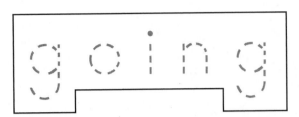

Help the boy get to the zoo.
Color each space that has
going. Use green.

Read. Circle each **going**.

We are going to the circus.

We are going to the zoo.

We are going to the fair.

You can come, too.

Write **going** to complete each sentence.

Are we _____ to the park?

Mom is _____ shopping today.

The Jumbo Book of Sight Word Practice Pages © 2013 by Immacula A. Rhodes, Scholastic Teaching Resources • page 273

Name: _____   Date: _____

going

Write **going**.

_____

- -

_____

Connect the dots to spell **going**.
Find the word two times.

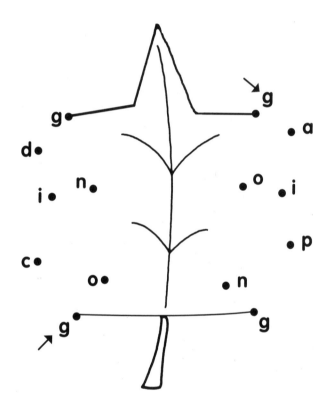

Write the missing letters
to spell **going**.

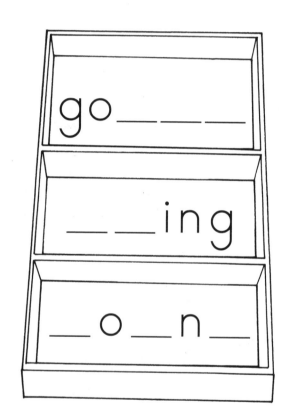

go _ _ _ _ _

_ _ ing

_ _ o _ n _

Color the boxes with the letters that spell **going**. Use orange.

b	c	j	m	g
p	a	i	n	d
g	o	l	w	q

d	o	t	u	b
g	e	i	m	g
q	c	j	n	p

Name: _____ Date: _____

Trace **walk** two times. Use red, then blue.

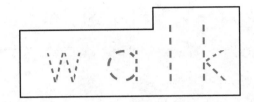

Color each apple that has **walk**.
Use red.

Read. Circle each **walk**.

This little bear took a walk through the apple trees. And on his walk, he picked lots of apples just for me.

Write **walk** to complete each sentence.

Let's _____ to the store.

I took a _____ after lunch.

Name: _____   Date: _____

Write **walk**.

_____

_ _

_____

Color each space that has **walk**.
Use yellow.

Write the missing letters
to spell **walk**.

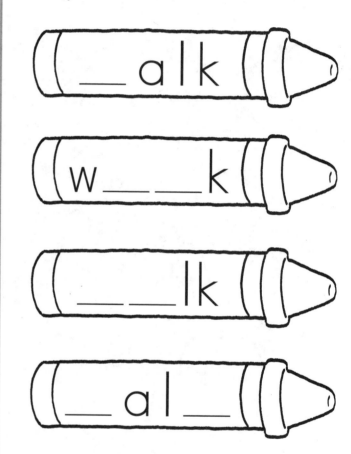

__a l k

w_____k

_____l k

__a l __

Color the glasses with the letters that spell **walk**. Use green.

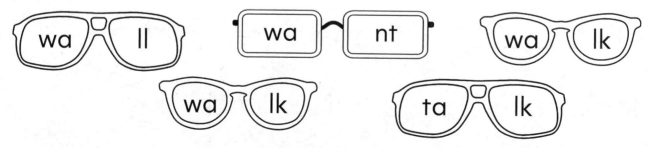

Name: _____   Date: _____

Trace **again** two times. Use red, then blue.

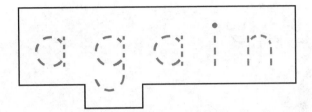

Color each bat that has **again** on both wings. Use gray.

Read. Circle each **again**.

One bat flew from a cave,

then flew back to it again.

One bat flew from a tree,

then flew back to it again.

Both bats flapped their

wings again and again

and again!

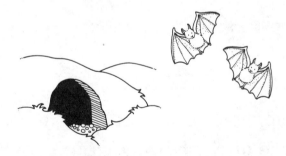

Write **again** to complete each sentence.

Play the drum _____, please.

The boat went by _____.

Name: _____   Date: _____

Write **again**.

_____

- - - - - - - - - - - - - - - - -

_____

Circle each **again**.
Find the word five times.

p a j m e t o
a g a i n c w
l a t c u a k
w i k o h g b
e n l b m a j
h p a g a i n
a g a i n n u

Color each balloon that has **again**. Draw a string from that balloon to the fence.

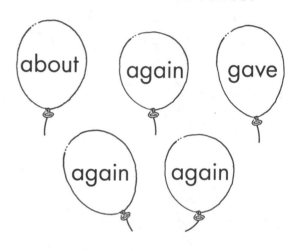

Help the chick get to the hen.
Trace the path with **again**.

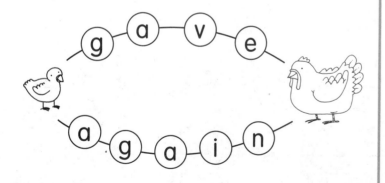

Write the missing letters to spell **again**.

a __ a i __

__ g __ i n

Name: _____   Date: _____

Trace **may** two times. Use red, then blue.

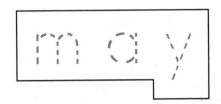

Color each space that has **may**.
Use orange.

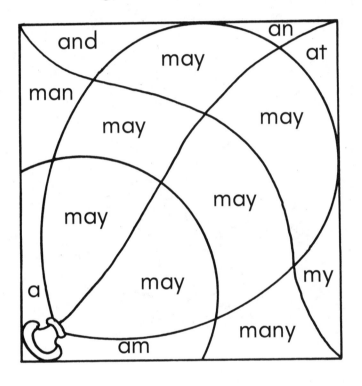

Read. Circle each **may**.

My balloon may be large.

My balloon may be small.

It may be the shape

of a big, round ball!

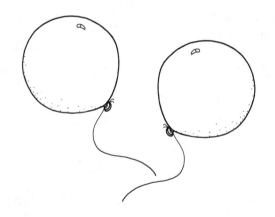

Write **may** to complete each sentence.

I _____ take a nap.

It _____ be hot outside.

Name: _____ Date: _____

Write **may**.

_____

_ _ _ _ _ _ _ _ _ _ _ _ _ _ _ _ _ _

_____

Find each flower that has **may**. Trace the path from that flower to the ladybug.

Write the missing letters to spell **may**.

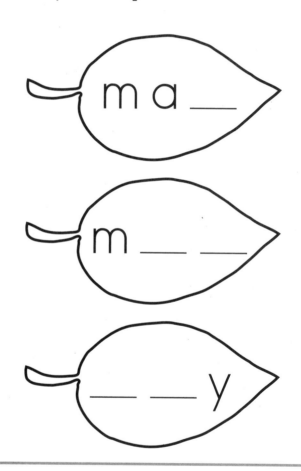

Color each set of bags with the letters that spell **may**. Use blue.

Name: _____   Date: _____

stop

Trace **stop** two times. Use red, then blue.

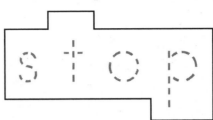

s t o p

Color each flag that has **stop**.
Use red.

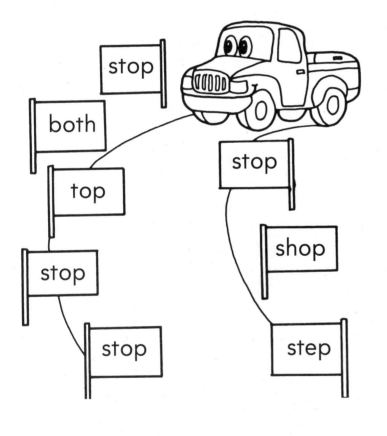

stop
both
top
stop
stop
stop
shop
step

Read. Circle each **stop**.

This truck will stop

at a stop sign.

This truck will stop

at a light.

This truck will stop

when it gets home,

so it can rest tonight.

Write **stop** to complete each sentence.

We must _____ at the sign.

She wants the rain to _____.

The Jumbo Book of Sight Word Practice Pages © 2013 by Immacula A. Rhodes, Scholastic Teaching Resources • page 281

Name: _____   Date: _____

stop

Write **stop**.

_____

_____

Circle each **stop**.
Find the word five times.

n g a s f s
f e s t n t
u s t o p o
s t o p u p
n a p e g n

Write the missing letters
to spell **stop**.

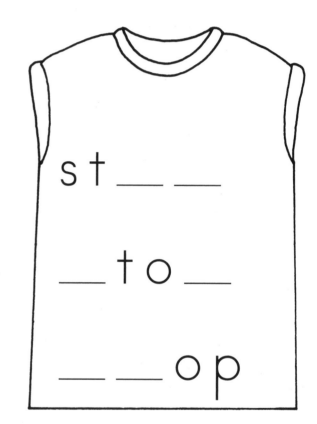

s t ___ ___

___ t o ___

___ ___ o p

Color each pair of apples with the letters that spell **stop**. Use green.

st op   st op   st ep   sh op

Name: _____ Date: _____

Trace **fly** two times. Use red, then blue.

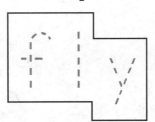

Color each space that has **fly**.
Use yellow.

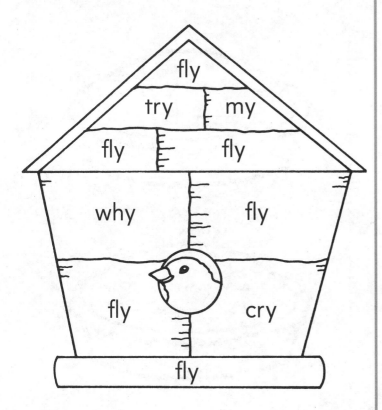

Read. Circle each **fly**.

Little bird, come out and fly.

Come fly right here to me.

How I wish I could fly.

Will you please teach me?

Write **fly** to complete each sentence.

My friend can _____ a plane.

There is a _____ in the room.

Name: _____ Date: _____

Write **fly**.

_____

- - - - - - - - - - - - - - - -

_____

Help each snowflake get to the ground. Connect the dots to spell **fly**. Start at **f**.

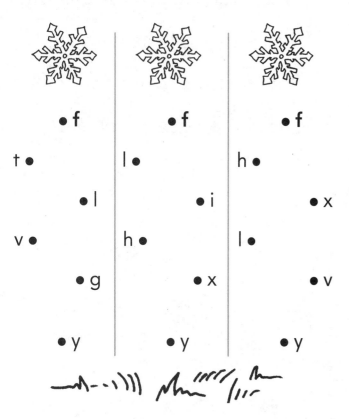

Write the missing letters to spell **fly**.

__ l y

f __ __

Color each banner that has **fly**. Use red.

| why | fly | fly | fry | my | fly | try | fly | cry |

The Jumbo Book of Sight Word Practice Pages © 2013 by Immacula A. Rhodes, Scholastic Teaching Resources • page 284

Name: _____   Date: _____

round

Trace **round** two times. Use red, then blue.

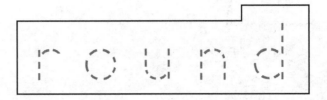

Help the kid get to the ball. Color each grass patch that has **round**. Use green.

Read. Circle each **round**.

A baseball is round.

A basketball is round.

A soccer ball is round.

But a football is *not* round.

Write **round** to complete each sentence.

The big wheel is _____.

This pie is in a _____ pan.

Name: _____   Date: _____

round

Write **round**.

_____

_ _ _ _ _ _ _ _ _ _ _ _ _

_____

Circle each **round**.
Find the word five times.

v r o u n d r
r o u n d v o
n u b a e p u
p n c w b a n
e d r o u n d

Write the missing letters
to spell **round**.

r _ _ _ n d

r o u _ _ _

r _ _ _ _ d

Color each pair of pears with the letters that spell **round**. Use yellow.

rou nd

cou ld

rou nd

wou ld

Name: _____ Date: _____

Trace **give** two times. Use red, then blue.

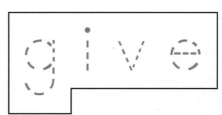

Color each cracker that has **give**.
Use yellow.

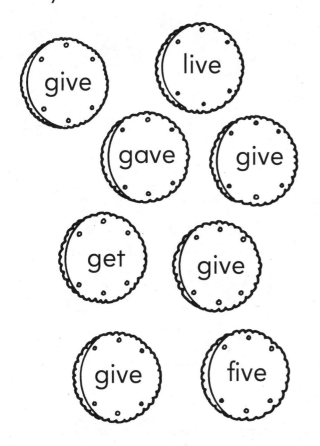

Read. Circle each **give**.

I'll give my bird one cracker.

I'll give him two or three.

And if he does not want any,

he'll give them back to me.

Write **give** to complete each sentence.

Will you _____ me a chip?

Please _____ the map to Dad.

Name: _____   Date: _____

give

Write **give**.

_____

- - - - - - - - - - - - - -

_____

Connect the dots to spell **give**.
Find the word two times.

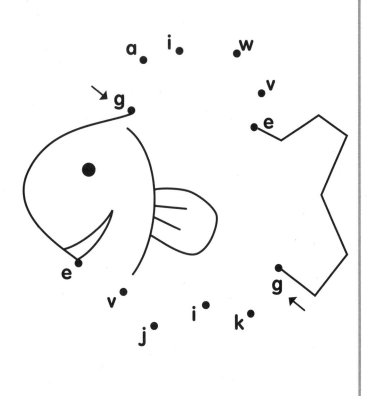

Write the missing letters
to spell **give**.

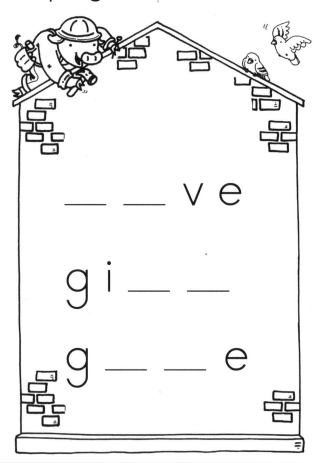

__ __ v e

g i __ __

g __ __ e

Color each pair of cookies with the letters that spell **give**. Use brown.

gi   ve

li   ve

gi   ve

Name: _____   Date: _____

Trace **once** two times. Use red, then blue.

Help the dragon get to the castle. Color each space that has **once**. Use yellow.

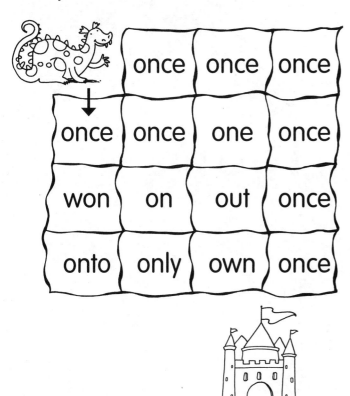

once	once	once
once	once	one	once
won	on	out	once
onto	only	own	once

Read. Circle each **once**.

I once lived in a castle.

A prince was once my friend.

I once met a big dragon.

But that was all pretend!

Write **once** to complete each sentence.

I rode a horse _____.

Our class _____ had a pet rabbit.

Name: _____   Date: _____

once

Write **once**.

_____

_ _

_____

Find each spider that has **once**.
Trace its path to the spout.

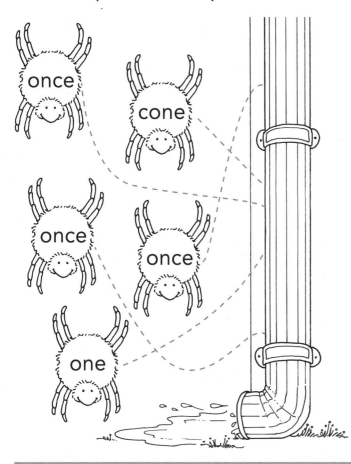

Write the missing letters
to spell **once**.

on_ _ _

o_ _ e

o_ c e

Circle each **once**.
Find the word five times.

w o n c e o
o n c e w n
u c v m a c
m e o n c e

Name: _____ Date: _____

Trace **open** two times. Use red, then blue.

Color each space that has **open**.
Use blue.

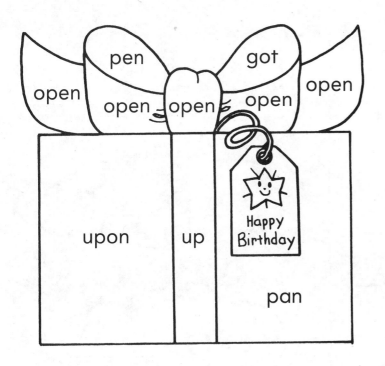

pen

got

open

open   open   open

open

upon   up   Happy Birthday

pan

Read. Circle each **open**.

It's time to open

the big gift.

Now, open the gift

that's small.

It's time to open

the long, thin gift.

It's time to open

them all!

Write **open** to complete each sentence.

Can we _____ the window?

This key will _____ the lock.

Name: _____   Date: _____

Write **open**.

_____

- - - - - - - - - - - - - - - - - -

_____

Help the horse get to the hay.
Trace the path that has **open**.

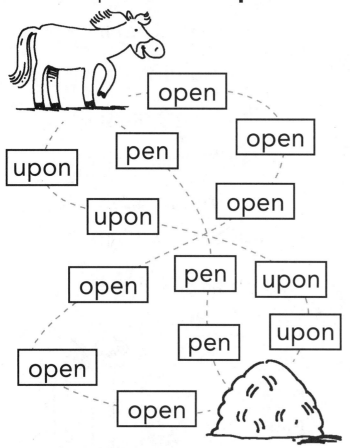

Write the missing letters
to spell **open**.

o __ e n

__ p __ n

o p __ __ __

Color each acorn that has **open**. Use brown.

pan

upon

open

open

open

Name: _____ Date: _____

has

Trace **has** two times. Use red, then blue.

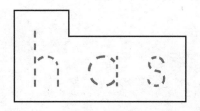

Color each space that has **has**.
Use yellow.

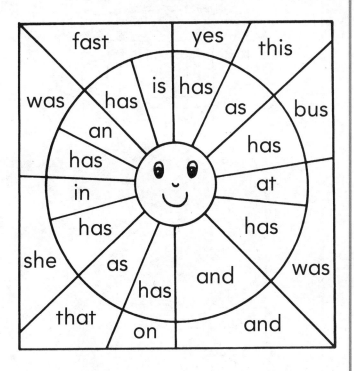

fast | yes | this | was | has | is | has | as | bus | an | has | at | has | in | has | she | as | and | was | that | has | on | and

Read. Circle each **has**.

The sun has come out.

It has chased the rain away.

It has dried everything.

We can now go out to play!

Write **has** to complete each sentence.

Our teacher _____ a new truck.

Pat _____ a dollar bill.

Name: _____ Date: _____

has

Write **has**.

_____

- - - - - - - - - -

_____

Find each deer that has **has**. Trace its path to the woods.

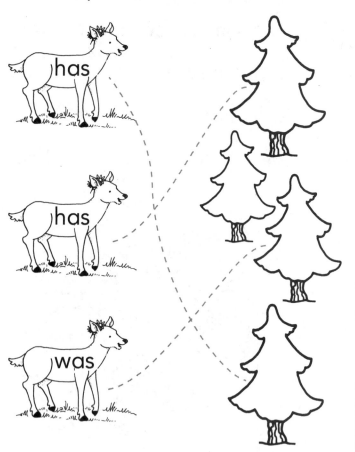

has

has

was

Write the missing letters to spell **has**.

__ a s

h a __

__ a __

Color each car with the letters that spell **has**. Use purple.

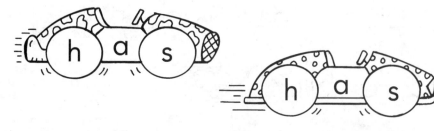

h a s

h a s

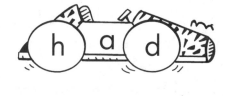

h a d

Name: _____   Date: _____

live

Trace **live** two times. Use red, then blue.

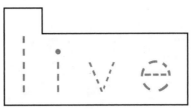

Color each space that has **live**. Use brown.

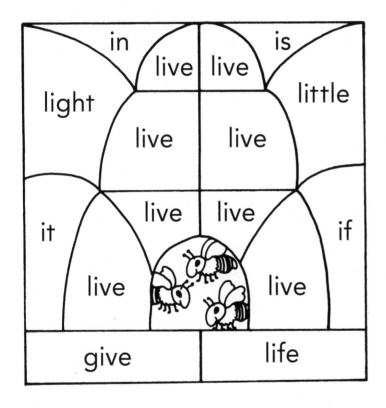

in	is
live	live
light	little
live	live
it	if
live	live
live	live
give	life

Read. Circle each **live**.

Some bugs live in holes.

Some bugs live in trees.

Some bugs live in hives—

and those bugs

would be bees!

Write **live** to complete each sentence.

Bats _____ in caves.

Which house do you _____ in?

Name: _____ Date: _____

live

Write **live**.

_____

- - - - - - - - - - - - - - - - - - - -

_____

Find each **live**.
Find the word five times.

f w j c l t
l i v e i l
i x t h v i
v j c w e v
e f l i v e

Write the missing letters
to spell **live**.

__ __ v e

l __ __ e

l i __ __

Color each clover that has the letters that spell **live**. Use green.

Name: _____ Date: _____

Trace **thank** two times. Use red, then blue.

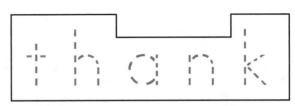

Help the teacher get to school.
Color each space that has **thank**.
Use red.

they	tank	think	thank
than	thank	thank	thank
	thank	that	their
→ thank	then	those

Read. Circle each **thank**.

We thank our helpers
at school.
We thank our helpers
in town.
We thank our helpers
everywhere.
We know they're always
around.

Write **thank** to complete each sentence.

Let's _____ Mom for the bike.

I want to _____ the dentist.

Name: _____   Date: _____

thank

Write **thank**.

_____

- - - - - - - - - - - - - - - - - - - -

_____

Circle each **thank**.
Find the word five times.

m	o	t	h	a	n	k
t	h	a	n	k	d	e
w	l	t	b	u	x	t
g	t	h	a	n	k	h
e	c	a	x	f	g	a
o	f	n	u	m	e	n
b	r	k	d	l	w	k

Help the lizard get to the rock.
Trace the path with **thank**.

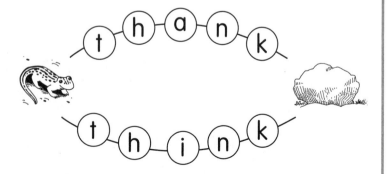

Color each kite that has
thank. Draw a string from
that kite to the kangaroo.

Write the missing letters
to spell **thank**.

t _ a _ _

_ _ _ n k

Name: _____ Date: _____

Trace **would** two times. Use red, then blue.

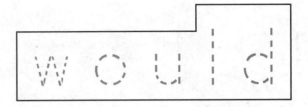

Color each space that has **would**. Use brown.

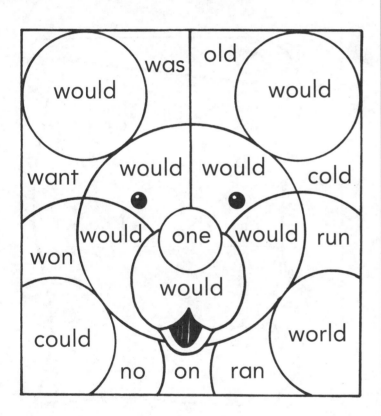

Read. Circle each **would**.

What would you do

if you worked at a zoo?

I would feed the bears.

Is that what you would do?

Write **would** to complete each sentence.

I _____ like some ice cream.

Where _____ you like the chair?

Name: _____ Date: _____

Write **would**.

_____

- - - - - - - - - - - - - - - - - -

_____

Help each giraffe get to its tree.
Trace the path with **would**.

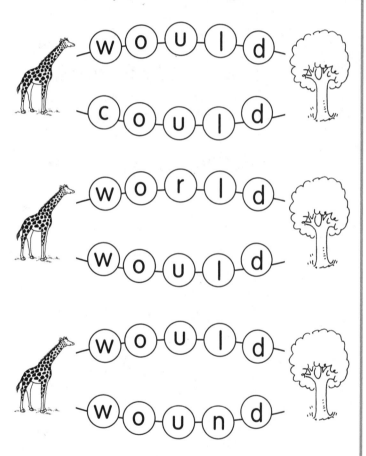

Write the missing letters
to spell **would**.

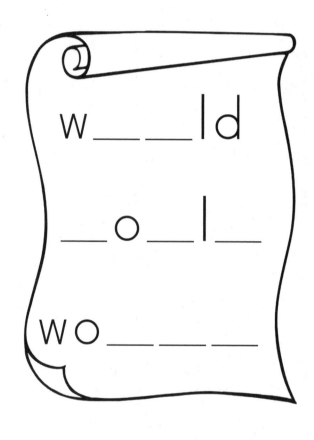

W _ _ _ l d

_ _ o _ l _

W o _ _ _ _

Color each turtle that has **would**. Use green.

would   would   could   world

Name: _____   Date: _____

very

Trace **very** two times. Use red, then blue.

Color each strawberry that has **very**. Use red.

Read. Circle each **very**.

When Mouse is very hungry,

she eats a strawberry.

Are you very hungry?

Yes—very, very, very!

Write **very** to complete each sentence.

The man has _____ big shoes.

This rope is _____ long.

Name: _____ Date: _____

Write **very**.

_____

- -

_____

Draw a line from each turtle to the puddle that has **very**.

 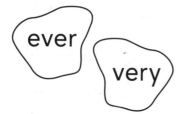

ever very

were very

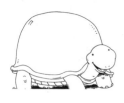 

very every

Write the missing letters to spell **very**.

__ery

___ry

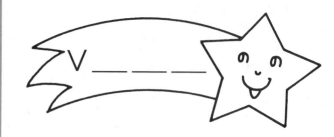

v____

Color each banner that has **very**. Use purple.

| were | ever | very | over | very | very | very | even | very |

Name: _____ Date: _____

your

Trace **your** two times. Use red, then blue.

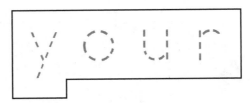

y o u r

Color each space that has **your**.
Use orange.

your | you
our | your
your | about
out
your
your

Read. Circle each **your**.

Let's hop on your boat

and put up your sail.

Does your boat sail fast,

or as slow as a snail?

Write **your** to complete each sentence.

May I use _____ tape?

Let's play _____ game today.

Name: _____ Date: _____

your

Write **your**.

_____

- - - - - - - - - - - - - -

_____

Connect the dots to spell **your**.
Find the word two times.

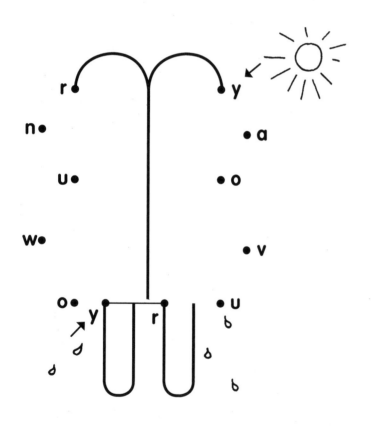

Write the missing letters
to spell **your**.

y ___ ___ ___ r

___ ___ ___ ___ r

Help the car get to the Finish line. Trace the path that has **your**.

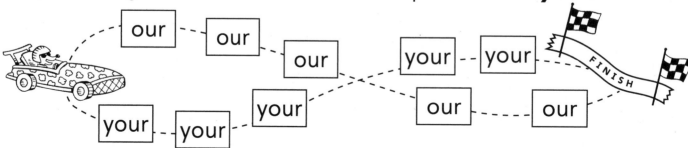

Name: _____   Date: _____

 Trace **its** two times. Use red, then blue.

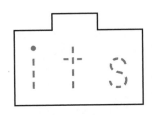

Color each space that has **its**.
Use yellow.

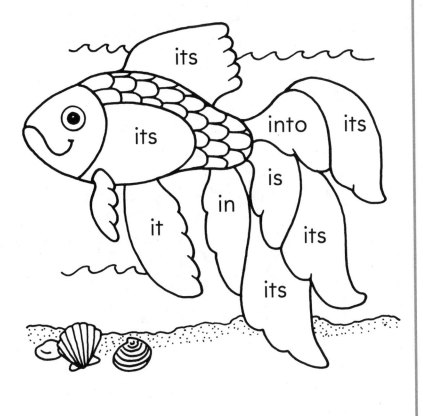

Read. Circle each **its**.

My fish flips its tail.

My fish flaps its fins.

My fish winks its eye.

Then away it swims.

Write **its** to complete each sentence.

The dog looked for _____ bone.

The ball is on _____ nose.

Name: _____   Date: _____

Write **its**.

_____

- -

_____

Help the rocket get to the moon.
Color each star that has **its**.
Use orange.

Write the missing letters
to spell **its**.

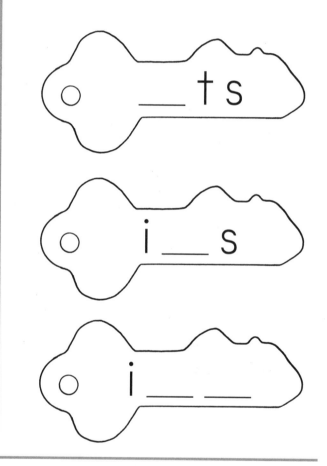

Color each set of balls with the letters that spell **its**. Use orange.

Name: _____   Date: _____

Trace **around** two times. Use red, then blue.

Color each space that has **around**. Use brown.

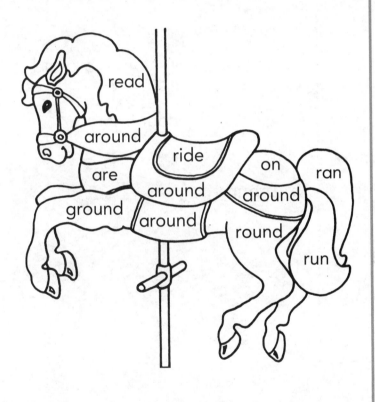

Read. Circle each **around**.

The red horse goes around.

The blue horse goes around.

All the horses go around

and around and around.

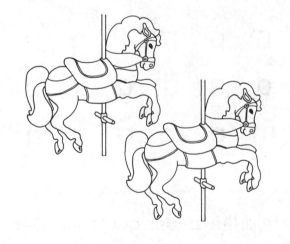

Write **around** to complete each sentence.

The ball rolled _____ the room.

We rode a bus _____ town.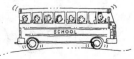

Name: _____ Date: _____

around

Write **around**.

_____

- -

_____

Circle each **around**.
Find the word five times.

a m a g c a v
r q r b e r a
o w o c p o r
u b u x w u o
n p n i q n u
d e d g k d n
m a r o u n d

Color each ice-cream scoop
that has **around**. Draw a line
from that scoop to a cone.

around   around

count

around   round

Help the spider get to the web.
Trace the path with **around**.

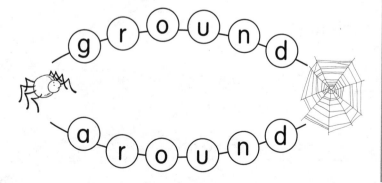

Write the missing letters
to spell **around**.

__ r __ __ n d

a __ o u __ __

The Jumbo Book of Sight Word Practice Pages © 2013 by Immacula A. Rhodes, Scholastic Teaching Resources • page 308

Name: _____ Date: _____

don't

Trace **don't** two times. Use red, then blue.

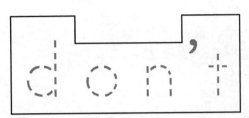

Color each space that has **don't**.
Use brown.

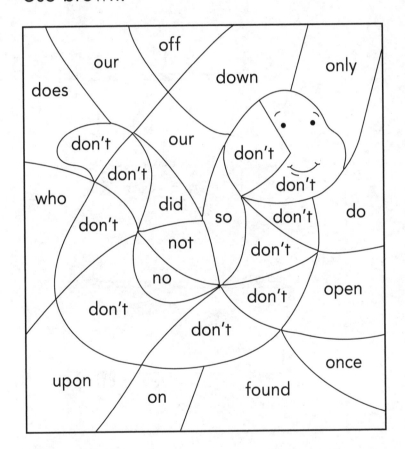

off
our
does
down
only
don't
our
don't
don't
who
did
so
don't
do
don't
not
no
don't
don't
open
don't
don't
once
upon
on
found

Read. Circle each **don't**.

I don't have arms.

I don't have hands.

I don't have legs.

I crawl on land.

What am I?

A worm!

Write **don't** to complete each sentence.

I _____ know why he is sad.

We _____ need this junk.

Name: _____ Date: _____

Write **don't**.

_____

_____

_____

Draw a line from each snake to the log that has **don't**.

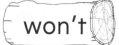
don't

won't

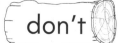
does

don't

down

don't

Write the missing letters to spell **don't**.

_____ n ' t

d _____ ' t

Color each pig that has **don't**. Use pink.

does

don't

down

don't

Name: _____ Date: _____

 right

Trace **right** two times. Use red, then blue.

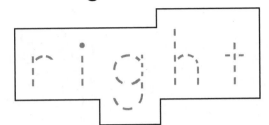

Color each space that has **right**.
Use orange.

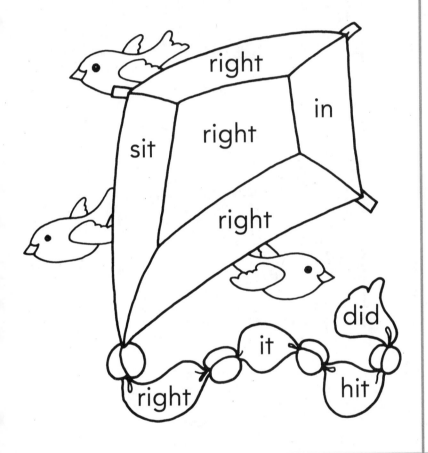

Read. Circle each **right**.

The weather is right.

The wind is right.

Let's go out right now

to fly our kite!

Write **right** to complete each sentence.

This is my _____ hand.

Is this the _____ bus?

Name: _____   Date: _____

right

Write **right**.

_____

_____

_____

Circle each **right**.
Find the word five times.

b	n	f	w	u	r
r	i	g	h	t	i
m	v	u	r	d	g
w	j	n	i	l	h
d	r	i	g	h	t
r	i	g	h	t	b
f	m	d	t	j	v

Write the missing letters
to spell **right**.

r ____ t

ri ____

____ ht

Color each bat with the letters that spell **right**. Use gray.

ri ght   ri ght   ni ght

The Jumbo Book of Sight Word Practice Pages © 2013 by Immacula A. Rhodes, Scholastic Teaching Resources • page 312

Name: _____ Date: _____

green

Trace **green** two times. Use red, then blue.

Color each space that has **green**. Use green.

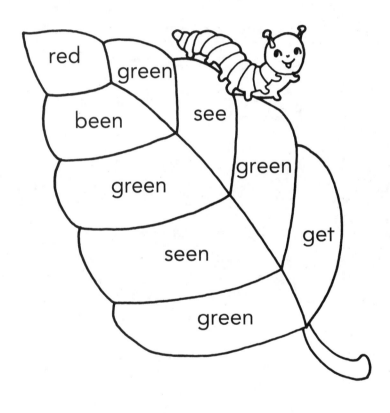

red

green

been

see

green

green

seen

get

green

Read. Circle each **green**.

The grass is green.

The plants are green.

And one green caterpillar

ate one green leaf.

Write **green** to complete each sentence.

Have some _____ grapes.

I have a _____ pet snake!

Name: _____ Date: _____

green

Write **green**.

_____

_____

_____

Help each bird get to its tree.
Trace the path that spells **green**.

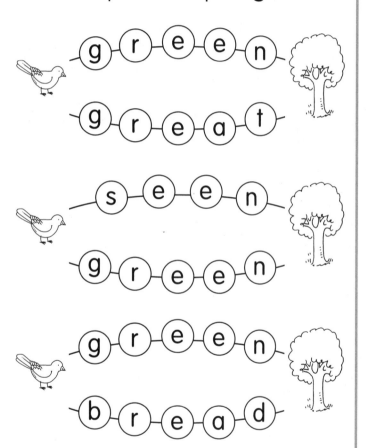

Write the missing letters
to spell **green**.

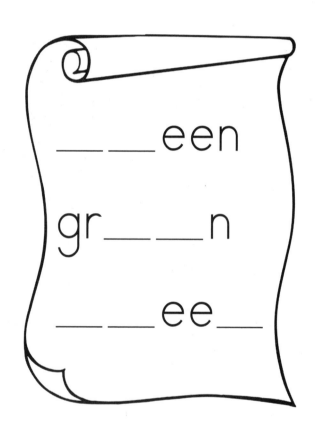

___een

gr___n

___ee__

Color each fish bowl that has **green**. Use green.

great   green   green   been   green

Name: _____ Date: _____

 their

Trace **their** two times. Use red, then blue.

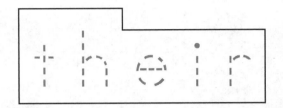

Color each petal that has **their**.
Use pink.

Read. Circle each **their**.

The kids plant their seeds

and watch them sprout.

They care for their plants

until flowers come out!

Write **their** to complete each sentence.

Our birds left _____ cage.

The kids rode _____ bikes.

Name: _____ Date: _____

their

Write **their**.

_____

- -

_____

Connect the dots to spell **their**.
Find the word two times.

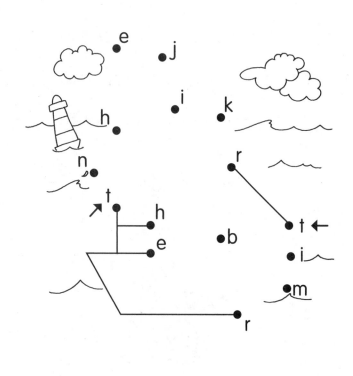

Write the missing letters
to spell **their**.

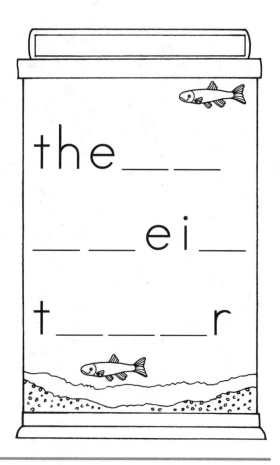

the___
___ei___
t____r

Color the two puzzle pieces with the letters that spell **their**. Use purple.

Name: _____ Date: _____

call

Trace **call** two times. Use red, then blue.

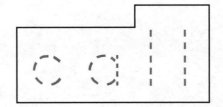

Color each shape that has **call**. Use yellow.

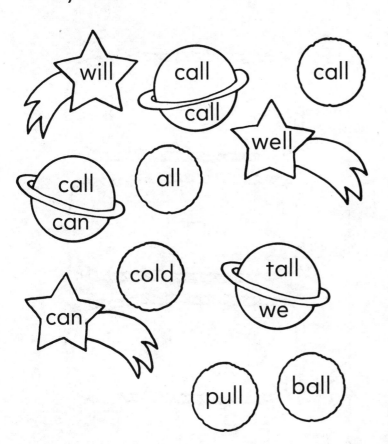

will call call call well call can all can cold tall we pull ball

Read. Circle each **call**.

We call stars bright.

We call planets round.

But when we see an alien,

we call anyone around!

Write **call** to complete each sentence.

I will _____ you on the phone.

Please, go _____ the dog.

Name: _____ Date: _____

call

Write **call**.

_____

- - - - - - - - - - - - - - - -

_____

Circle each **call**.
Find the word five times.

e c a l l s
g a f c u h
h l c a l l
u l t l g e
c a l l f t

Write the missing letters
to spell **call**.

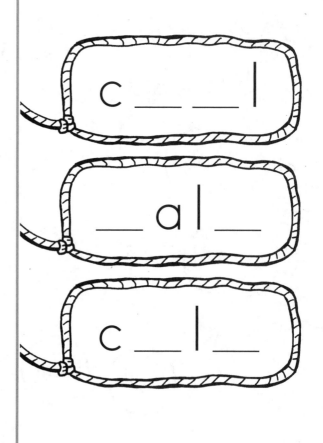

c _ _ l

_ a l _

c _ _ l

Color each pair of cows with the letters that spell **call**. Use gray.

ta ll   ca ll   ca ll   ba ll

Name: _____   Date: _____

sleep

Trace **sleep** two times. Use red, then blue.

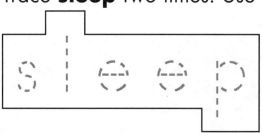

Color each space that has **sleep**. Use brown.

Read. Circle each **sleep**.

When the sun wakes up,

Little Owl will sleep.

Owls sleep when it is light.

When the sun goes to sleep,

Little Owl wakes up.

Owls do not sleep at night.

Write **sleep** to complete each sentence.

The dog went to _____.

How long did he _____?

Name: _____   Date: _____

Write **sleep**.

_____

_____

_____

Draw a line from each frog to the lily pad that has **sleep**.

 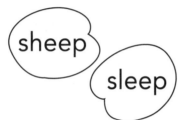
sheep
sleep

steep
sleep

sleep
keep

Write the missing letters to spell **sleep**.

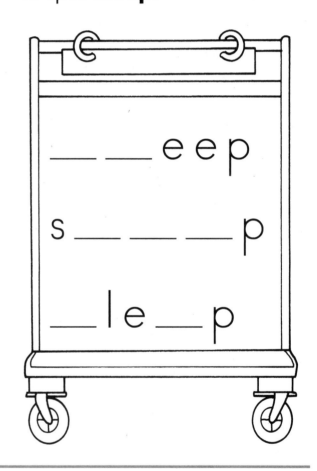

_ _ _ e e p

s _ _ _ _ p

_ l e _ p

Color the boxes with the letters that spell **sleep**. Use orange.

q	h	e	a	d
s	l	c	e	g
x	f	o	u	p

r	t	a	o	b
g	l	u	e	p
s	f	e	c	d

Name: _____ Date: _____

 **five**

Trace **five** two times. Use red, then blue.

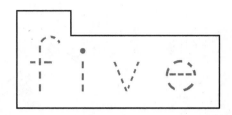

Color each owl that has **five**.
Use yellow.

five · find · five · live

fill · five · five · first

Read. Circle each **five**.

There once was five owls

sitting in a row.

They saw five mice go by.

Go, mice, go!

Write **five** to complete each sentence.

The hen laid _____ eggs.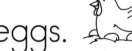

The man cut _____ logs.

Name: _____ Date: _____

five

Write **five**.

_____

- -

_____

Help each sheep get to its barn.
Trace the path with **five**.

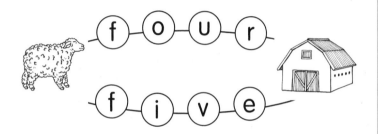
f o u r
f i v e

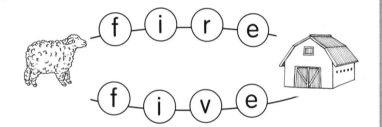
f i r e
f i v e

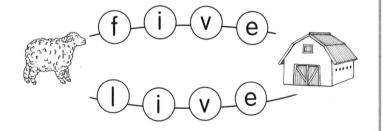
f i v e
l i v e

Write the missing letters
to spell **five**.

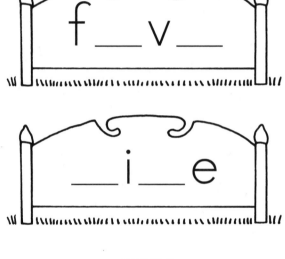
f __ v __

__ i __ e

f __ __ __ __

Color each bird that has **five**. Use red.

fire   five   file   five

The Jumbo Book of Sight Word Practice Pages © 2013 by Immacula A. Rhodes, Scholastic Teaching Resources • page 322

Name: _____   Date: _____

Trace **wash** two times. Use red, then blue.

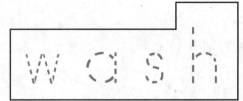

Color each mitten that has **wash**. Use purple.

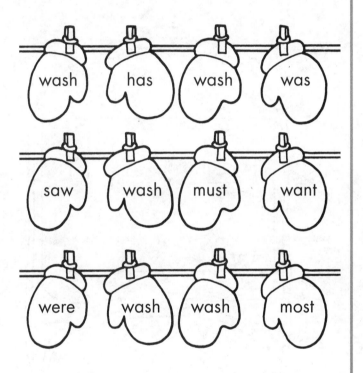

wash   has   wash   was

saw   wash   must   want

were   wash   wash   most

Read. Circle each **wash**.

Mouse, will you wash

our mittens?

Will you wash them very well?

And after you wash

our mittens,

we'll put them out to sell.

Write **wash** to complete each sentence.

I need to _____ this shirt.

Mom wants to _____ the car.

Name: _____ Date: _____

Write **wash**.

_____

- - - - - - - - - - - - - - -

_____

Help each crow get to the corn. Connect the dots to spell **wash**. Start at **w**.

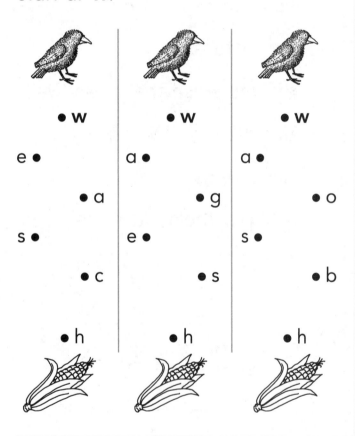

Write the missing letters to spell **wash**.

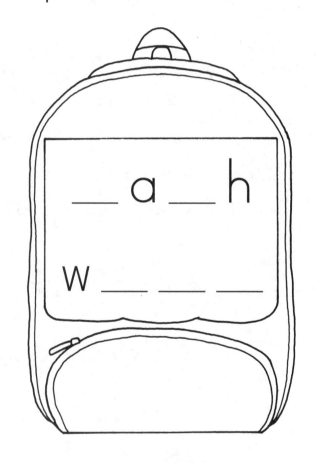

_ a _ h

W _ _ _

Color each train car that has **wash**. Use red.

| was | wash | want | wash | wash |

Name: _____   Date: _____

Trace **or** two times. Use red, then blue.

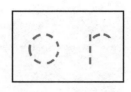

Color each space that has **or**.
Use blue.

Read. Circle each **or**.

Is Cat wearing stripes,

or a lot of polka dots?

Are his pajamas warm,

or are they very hot?

Is Cat ready for bed,

or is he not?

Write **or** to complete each sentence.

Do you want cake _____ pie?

I don't have paper _____ a pencil.

Name: _____   Date: _____

Write **or** two times.

_____   _____

_____   _____

_____   _____

Find each berry that has **or**.
Trace the path from that berry
to the bear.

Write **or** on each fish.

Color each pair of music notes with the letters that spell **or**. Use purple.

Name: _____   Date: _____

 before

Trace **before** two times. Use red, then blue.

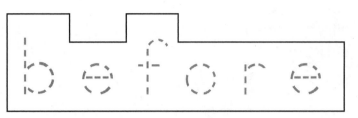

Color each space that has **before**. Use brown.

before
because
before
began
be
before
belong
before

Read. Circle each **before**.

One beaver rests

before it gets to work.

One beaver works

before it gets to rest.

Rest before work.

Work before rest.

And before you know it,

the beavers have a home!

Write **before** to complete each sentence.

Let's eat _____ we go.

Please rest _____ the race.

Name: _____   Date: _____

before

Write **before**.

_____

- - - - - - - - - - - - - - - - - -

_____

Circle each **before**.
Find the word five times.

a	b	c	v	u	b	a
b	e	f	o	r	e	b
o	f	k	t	g	f	e
w	o	c	a	d	o	f
g	r	e	w	k	r	o
b	e	f	o	r	e	r
a	d	u	v	c	t	e

Color each balloon that has **before**. Draw a string from that balloon to the fence.

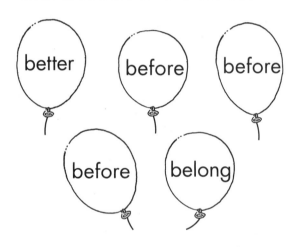

Help the chick get to the hen.
Trace the path with **before**.

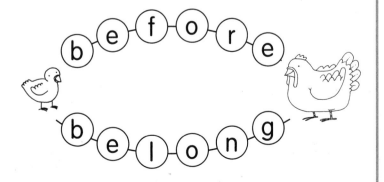

Write the missing letters
to spell **before**.

be___ ___e

___ ___for___

Name: _____ Date: _____

 **been**

Trace **been** two times. Use red, then blue.

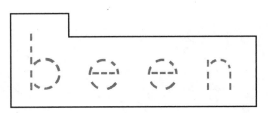

Color each space that has **been**. Use yellow.

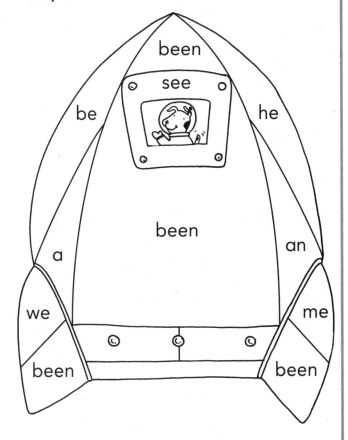

Read. Circle each **been**.

Puppy has been to the stars.

Puppy has been to the moon.

Puppy has been in space.

I hope to go there soon.

Write **been** to complete each sentence.

We have _____ in the rain.

Have you _____ home yet?

Name: _____ Date: _____

been

Write **been**.

_____

_ _ _ _ _ _ _ _ _ _ _ _ _ _ _

_____

Circle each **been**.
Find the word five times.

b o b e e n

e v a b o b

e m d e c e

n b e e n e

w o d n u n

Write the missing letters
to spell **been**.

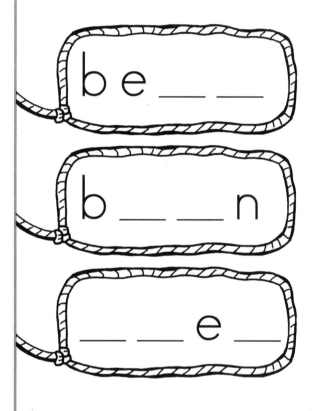

b e ___ ___

b ___ ___ n

___ ___ e ___

Color each bear that has **been**. Use brown.

been   her   been   been   ten   be

Name: _____ Date: _____

Trace **off** two times. Use red, then blue.

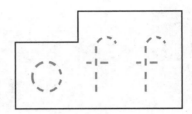

Help the bird get to the ground.
Color each cloud with **off**.
Use blue.

Read. Circle each **off**.

I saw a fish,

and the fish swam off.

I saw a bird,

and the bird flew off.

I saw my friend,

and we both ran off to play!

Write **off** to complete each sentence.

The turtle is _____ the rock.

I took my shoes _____.

Name: _____ Date: _____

Write **off**.

_____

- -

_____

Find each fish that has **off**.
Trace its path to the water.

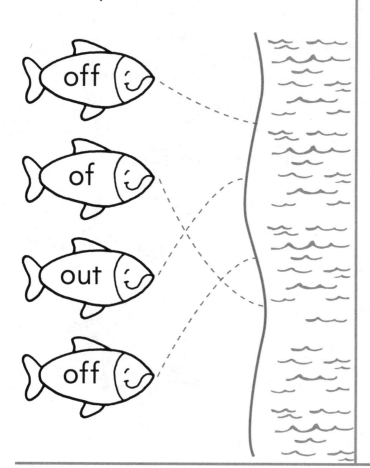

Write the missing letters
to spell **off**.

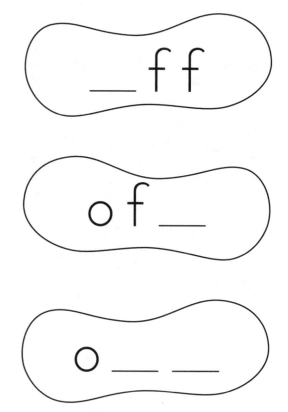

Color each flower with the letters that spell **off**. Use yellow.

o f f   o u t   o f f   f o r

Name: _____ Date: _____

Trace **cold** two times. Use red, then blue.

cold

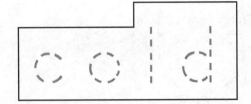

Color each penguin that has **cold**. Use gray.

cold   cold   old   cold

gold   good   cold   could

Read. Circle each **cold**.

Penguins live in the cold.

Penguins eat in the cold.

Penguins play in the cold.

Penguins even swim

in the cold!

Write **cold** to complete each sentence.

The snow is very _____.

A _____ wind is blowing.

Name: _____   Date: _____

Write **cold**.

_____

- - - - - - - - - - - - - - -

_____

Circle each **cold**.
Find the word five times.

c   o   l   d
o   b   t   c
l   f   a   o
d   e   c   l
u   t   o   d
c   o   l   d
g   a   d   f

Write the missing letters
to spell **cold**.

c o __ d

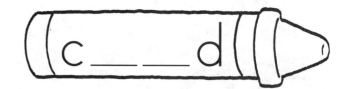

c __ __ d

__ __ l d

Help the mouse get to the cheese. Trace the path that has **cold**.

cold — cold — cold

old — old

old — old — cold — cold

Name: _____ Date: _____

Trace **tell** two times. Use red, then blue.

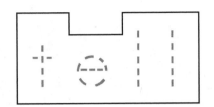

Color each space that has **tell**.
Use brown.

Read. Circle each **tell**.

Where is the shell?

Will you please tell?

Is it up or down?

Is it on the ground?

Where is the shell?

Do tell, please tell!

Write **tell** to complete each sentence.

I can _____ the time.

Go _____ Mom that I'm sick.

Name: _____ Date: _____

Write **tell**.

_____

- - - - - - - - - - - - - - - - - - -

_____

Help each raindrop get to the ground.
Connect the dots to spell **tell**.
Start at **t**.

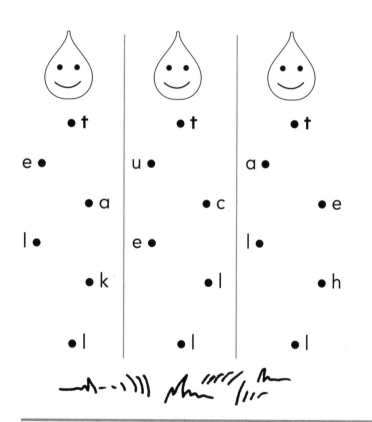

Write the missing letters
to spell **tell**.

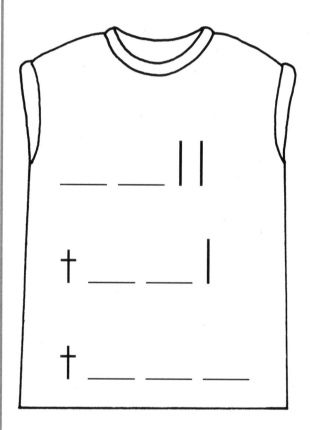

Color each robot that has **tell**. Use yellow.

then   tell   tell   tall

The Jumbo Book of Sight Word Practice Pages © 2013 by Immacula A. Rhodes, Scholastic Teaching Resources • page 336

Name: _____   Date: _____

Trace **work** two times. Use red, then blue.

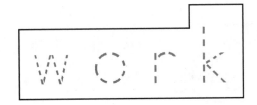

Color each space that has **work**. Use yellow.

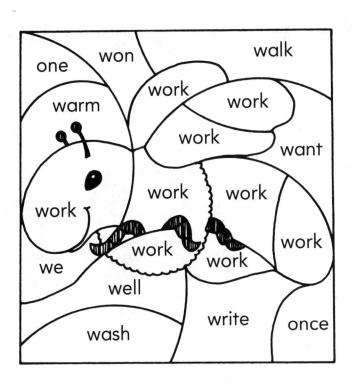

one
won
walk
warm
work
work
work
want
work
work
work
work
we
work
work
well
write
once
wash

Read. Circle each **work**.

Bees work hard.

They work each day.

Bees work hard—

no time for play.

Write **work** to complete each sentence.

Mom drives a van to _____.

We _____ together as a team.

The Jumbo Book of Sight Word Practice Pages © 2013 by Immacula A. Rhodes, Scholastic Teaching Resources • page 337

Name: _____ Date: _____

Write **work**.

_____

- -

_____

Find each frog that has **work**.
Trace its path to the water.

Write the missing letters
to spell **work**.

w _ _ _ k

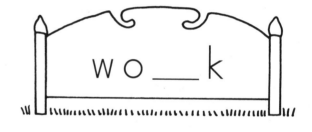

w o _ _ k

_ _ _ r k

Color each pair of trees with the letters that spell **work**. Use green.

wo rk

wa nt

wr ite

wo rk

Name: _____ Date: _____

first

Trace **first** two times. Use red, then blue.

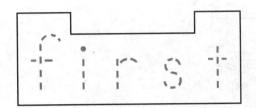

Color each space that has **first**.
Use red.

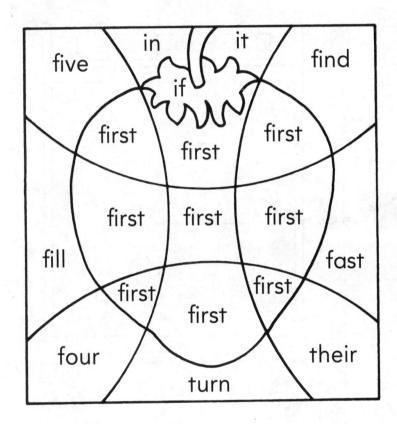

Read. Circle each **first**.

I made my first trip
to a strawberry patch.
I picked the first
strawberry I saw.
Then I ate the first
strawberry I picked.
Yum! Yum!

Write **first** to complete each sentence.

I used the swing _____.

The girl won _____ place.

Name: _____ Date: _____

Write **first**.

_____

- - - - - - - - - - - - - - - -

_____

Draw a line from each frog to the lily pad that has **first**.

first

find

first

five

 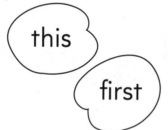

this

first

Write the missing letters to spell **first**.

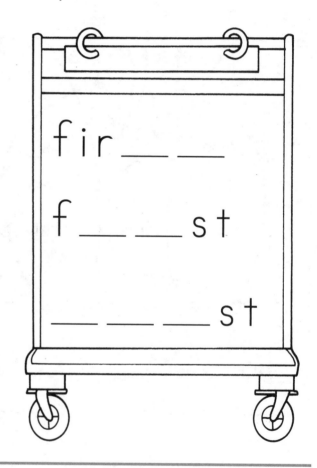

f i r _ _ _

f _ _ _ s t

_ _ _ _ s t

Color the boxes with the letters that spell **first**. Use red.

f	i	n	x	k
h	l	r	s	b
d	j	u	c	t

h	j	r	g	l
b	i	m	s	x
f	k	w	q	t

Name: _____ Date: _____

does

Trace **does** two times. Use red, then blue.

Help the bat get to the cave.
Color each space that has **does**.
Use brown.

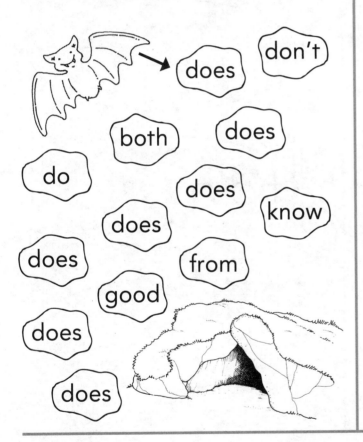

does
don't
both
does
do
does
does
know
does
from
good
does
does

Read. Circle each **does**.

Where does a bat live?

How does it get about?

What does a bat eat?

Read a book to find out!

Write **does** to complete each sentence.

How much _____ the boat cost?

What _____ a cow eat?

Name: _____ Date: _____

does

Write **does**.

_____

- -

_____

Help the train get to the track.
Trace the path that has **does**.

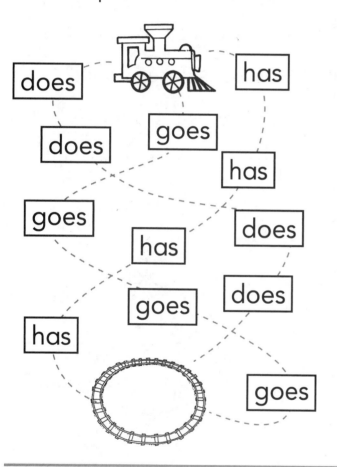

Write the missing letters
to spell **does**.

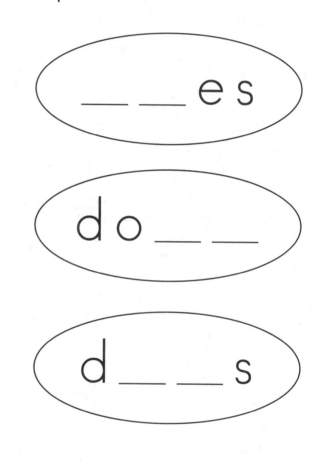

___ ___ e s

d o ___ ___

d ___ ___ s

Color each part of the snake that has **does**. Use orange.

does does has does does goes do

Name: _____   Date: _____

Trace **goes** two times. Use red, then blue.

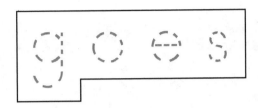

Help the girl get home. Color each space that has **goes**. Use red.

goes	get	yes
gave	goes	done	your
does	goes	goes	help
go	you	goes	got

Read. Circle each **goes**.

The girl goes

around the house.

The girl goes

up the street.

Then she goes back home

to get a yummy treat.

Write **goes** to complete each sentence.

The book _____ in the bag.

Tim _____ to the park each day.

Name: _____   Date: _____

goes

Write **goes**.

_____

- - - - - - - - - - - - - - - - - -

_____

Help each cat get to its yarn.
Trace the path with **goes**.

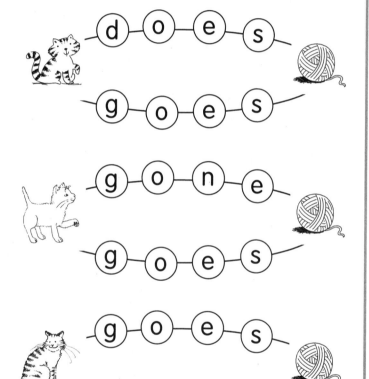

Write the missing letters
to spell **goes**.

g __ __ s

g o __ __ __

__ __ e s

Color each pair of peas with the letters that spell **goes**. Use green.

go es   go ne   go es

Name: _____   Date: _____

write

Trace **write** two times. Use red, then blue.

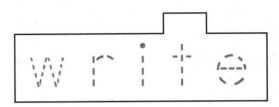

Color each pencil that has **write**. Use red.

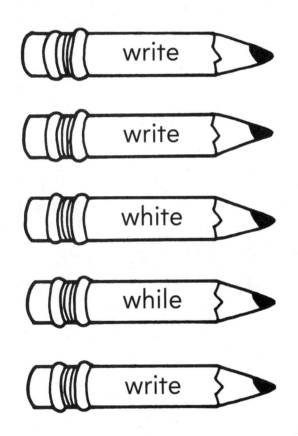

write

write

white

while

write

Read. Circle each **write**.

I like to write about flowers.

I like to write about bees.

I like to write about

sunny days.

I like to write about me!

Write **write** to complete each sentence.

Use a pencil to _____.

I want to _____ a story.

Name: _____   Date: _____

write

Write **write**.

_____

- -

_____

Find each boat that has **write**. Trace the path from that boat to the dock.

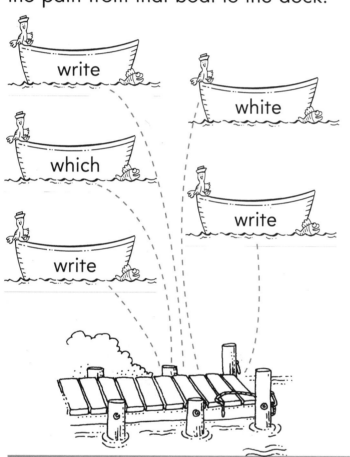

Write the missing letters to spell **write**.

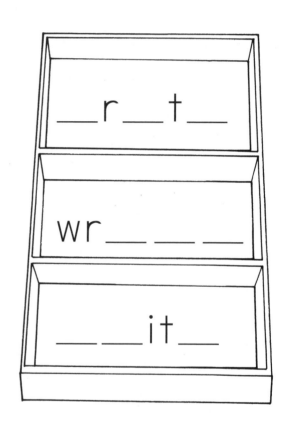

__ r __ t __

wr __ __ __ __

__ __ it __

Color the boxes with the letters that spell **write**. Use blue.

v	x	k	t	e
n	u	i	l	g
w	r	j	h	s

m	r	j	h	c
w	k	i	l	e
v	n	l	t	a

Name: _____   Date: _____

always

Trace **always** two times. Use red, then blue.

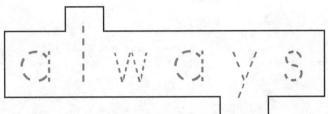

always

Color each flower that has **always**. Use pink.

around | always | always | away

always | again | always | after

Read. Circle each **always**.

Butterflies always fly,

grass always turns green,

flowers always bloom

in the nice, warm days

of spring.

Write **always** to complete each sentence.

My shoes are _____ untied.

I _____ have grapes at lunch.

Name: _____ Date: _____

always

Write **always**.

_____

_____

_____

Circle each **always**.
Find the word five times.

t a l w a y s
a l w a y s e
o w u l g f v
h a l w a y s
k y u a t h o
e s c y u g x
v o x s f k e

Help the squirrel get to the tree.
Trace the path with **always**.

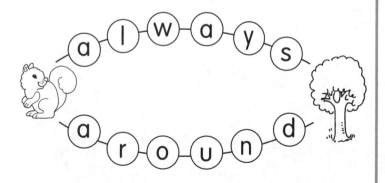

Color each ice-cream scoop
that has **always**. Draw a line
from that scoop to a cone.

Write the missing letters
to spell **always**.

a l __ __ __ s

__ __ w a y __

The Jumbo Book of Sight Word Practice Pages © 2013 by Immacula A. Rhodes, Scholastic Teaching Resources • page 348

Name: _____   Date: _____

made

Trace **made** two times. Use red, then blue.

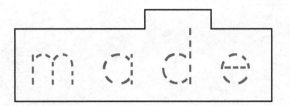

Color each space that has **made**.
Use red.

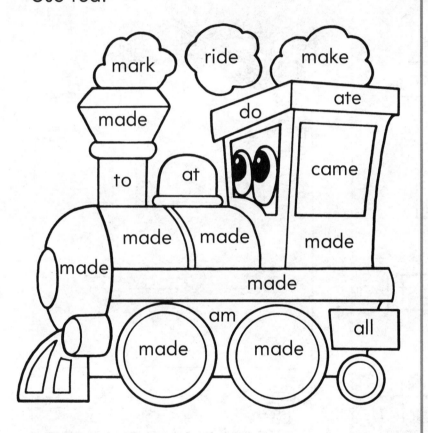

mark   ride   make
made   do   ate
to   at   came
made   made   made
made
am   all
made   made

Read. Circle each **made**.

We made a trip

on a train.

We made the trip

in the rain.

Write **made** to complete each sentence.

The bees _____ a hive.

Who _____ this mess?

Name: _____   Date: _____

made

Write **made**.

_____

- -

_____

Help the cat get to the mouse.
Trace the path that has **made**.

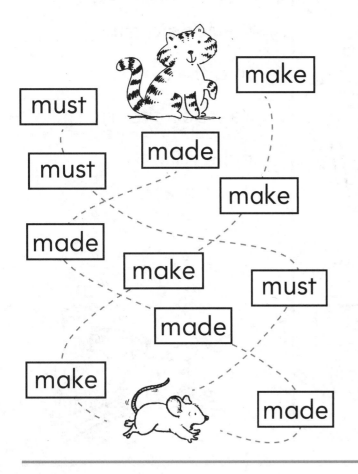

must

must

made

make

make

make

make

must

made

made

Write the missing letters
to spell **made**.

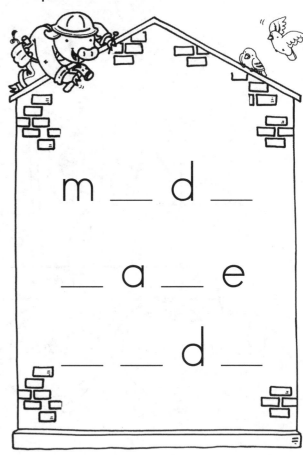

m __ d __

__ a __ e

d

__ __ d __

Color each pair of cupcakes with the letters that spell **made**. Use pink.

ya rd

ma de

ma ke

ma de

Name: _____   Date: _____

gave

Trace **gave** two times. Use red, then blue.

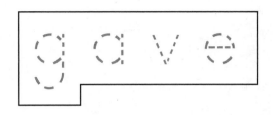

Help the kid get to the piggy bank. Color each space that has **gave**. Use yellow.

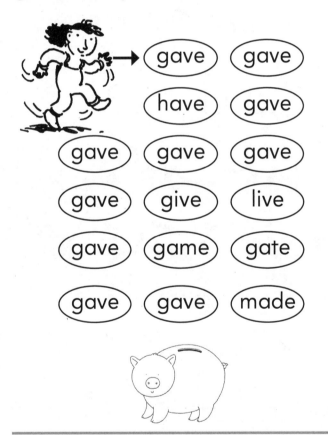

gave	gave
have	gave
gave	gave	gave
gave	give	live
gave	game	gate
gave	gave	made

Read. Circle each **gave**.

Mom gave me a nickel.

Dad gave me a dime.

I gave them both

a great big thanks,

then gave the coins

to my piggy bank!

Write **gave** to complete each sentence.

I _____ away my flower.

The teacher _____ us cookies.

Name: _____   Date: _____

gave

Write **gave**.

_____

- -

_____

Find each leaf that has **gave**.
Trace the path from that leaf
to the basket.

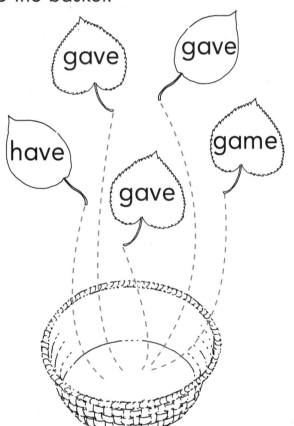

Write the missing letters
to spell **gave**.

Color the two socks with the letters that spell **gave**. Use purple.

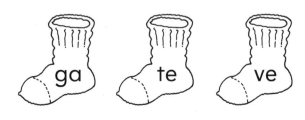

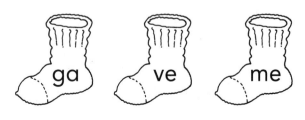

Name: _____ Date: _____

Trace **us** two times. Use red, then blue.

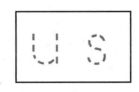

Color each space that has **us**.
Use yellow.

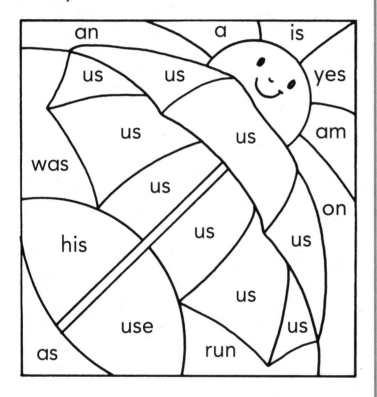

Read. Circle each **us**.

The rain fell on us.

It made us very wet.

Dad gave us an umbrella,

but we have not used it yet!

Write **us** to complete each sentence.

A frog hopped by _____.

Come join _____ on our hike.

Name: _____   Date: _____

us

Write **us** two times.

_____   _____

_____   _____

Find each mushroom that has **us**.
Trace the path from that mushroom
to the mouse.

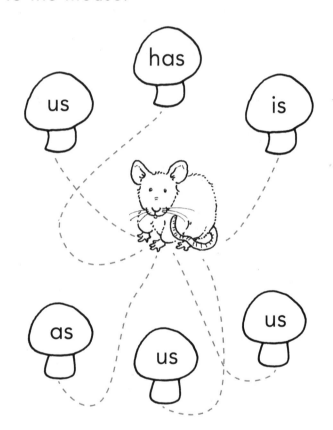

has

us

is

as

us

us

Write **us** on each clover.

U S

___ ___

___ ___

___ ___

___ ___

Color each pair of friends with the letters that spell **us**. Use blue.

a s   u s   u s   i s

Name: _____   Date: _____

Trace **buy** two times. Use red, then blue.

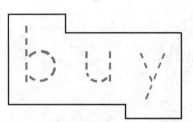

Help the man get to store.
Color each space that has **buy**.
Use blue.

why	they	buy	my
way	by	buy	buy
	may	but	buy
buy	buy	buy	buy

Read. Circle each **buy**.

Please buy me a book.

Please buy me a ball.

Please buy me a boat.

Please go buy them all.

Write **buy** to complete each sentence.

I have a dollar to _____ gum.

We need to _____ milk.

Name: _____ Date: _____

Write **buy**.

_____

- -

_____

Find each fox that has **buy**.
Trace its path to the woods.

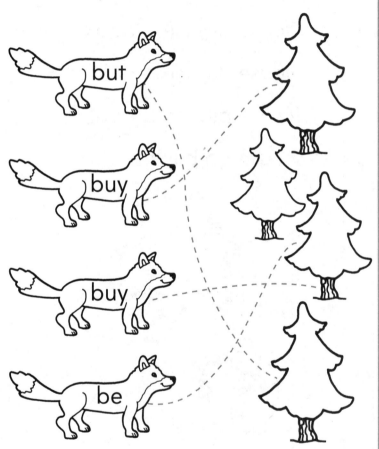

Write the missing letters
to spell **buy**.

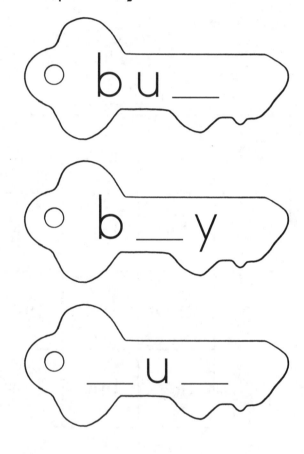

b u ___

b ___ y

___ u ___

Circle each **buy**.
Find the word five times.

b u y d o h
u d a e b a
y e x b u y
w a b u y v

Name: _____   Date: _____

 those

Trace **those** two times. Use red, then blue.

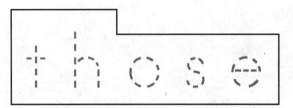

Color each shell that has **those**. Use yellow.

those
these
whose
those
does
there
those
those

Read. Circle each **those**.

The crab wants

those seashells.

He wants those shells, too.

But those shells

are not for him.

They are for me and you!

Write **those** to complete each sentence.

Where are _____ mice?

Let's plant _____ seeds.

Name: _____   Date: _____

Write **those**.

_____

- -

_____

Color each kite that has **those**. Draw a string from that kite to the kangaroo.

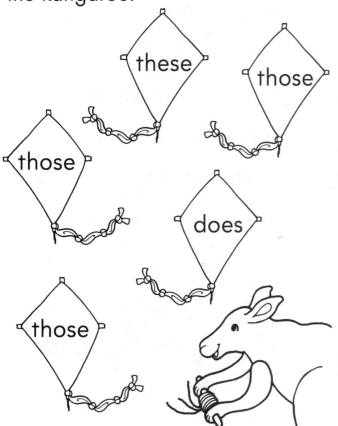

Write the missing letters to spell **those**.

___ ___ o s e

t ___ ___ ___ ___ e

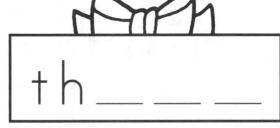

t h ___ ___ ___ ___

Color each pair of apples with the letters that spell **those**. Use green.

th ose   th em   th ese   th ose

Name: _____   Date: _____

use

Trace **use** two times. Use red, then blue.

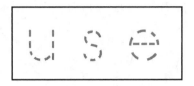

Color each space that has **use**.
Use red.

Read. Circle each **use**.

We use fire to cook.

We use fire for light.

We use fire for many things,

but we must always

use it right.

Write **use** to complete each sentence.

I will _____ the phone now.

You _____ a broom to sweep.

Name: _____   Date: _____

use

Write **use**.

_____

_____

_____

Connect the dots to spell **use**.
Find the word two times.

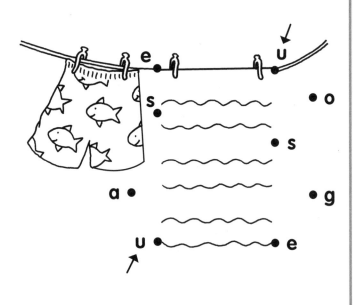

Write the missing letters
to spell **use**.

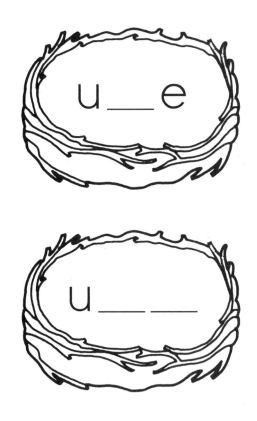

u___e

u_____

Color each owl that has **use**. Use brown.

us   use   up   use   use   our   use   an

Name: _____   Date: _____

fast

Trace **fast** two times. Use red, then blue.

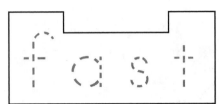

Color each rocket that has **fast**.
Use purple.

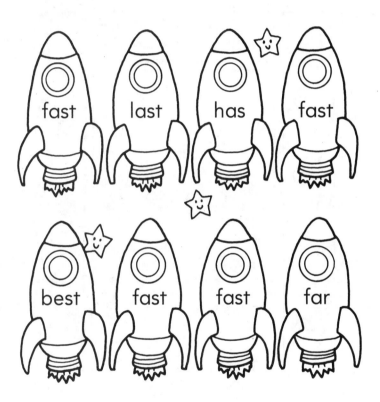

Read. Circle each **fast**.

A rocket goes fast.

It goes fast and far.

A rocket goes fast

as it heads for the stars.

Write **fast** to complete each sentence.

The boy can run _____.

She threw the ball _____.

Name: _____   Date: _____

fast

Write **fast**.

_____

_____

_____

Help the pig get to its ribbon.
Trace the path that has **fast**.

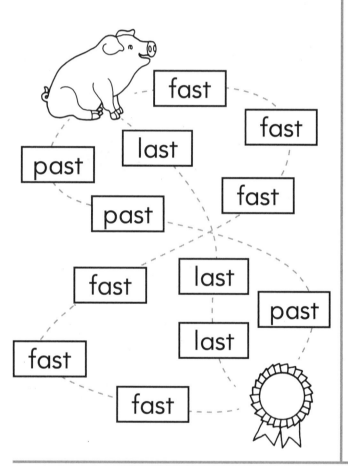

fast

fast

last

past

fast

past

fast

last

past

fast

last

fast

Write the missing letters
to spell **fast**.

f ___ ___ t

___ a s ___

___ ___ ___ ___ t

Color each pair of clouds with the letters that spell **fast**. Use gray.

fa
st

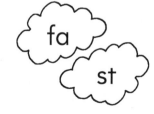

fa
st

fa
ll

fa
ir

Name: _____   Date: _____

pull

Trace **pull** two times. Use red, then blue.

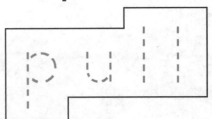

Help the dog get to the wagon. Color each grass patch that has **pull**. Use green.

Read. Circle each **pull**.

You can pull a log.

You can pull a dog.

Just put it in your wagon

and pull it all day long.

Write **pull** to complete each sentence.

I want to _____ the sled.

Help me _____ off my glove.

Name: _____ Date: _____

pull

Write **pull**.

_____

- -

_____

Find each frog that has **pull**.
Trace its path to the water.

tell

push

pull

pull

Write the missing letters
to spell **pull**.

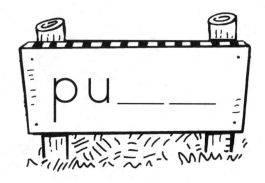

p u _____

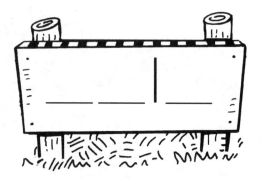

_____ l _____

Color each pair of trees with the letters that spell **pull**. Use green.

pu   sh

pu   ll

fa   ll

pu   ll

The Jumbo Book of Sight Word Practice Pages © 2013 by Immacula A. Rhodes, Scholastic Teaching Resources • page 364

Name: _____   Date: _____

Trace **both** two times. Use red, then blue.

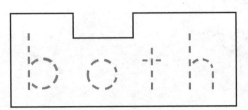

Color each ball that has **both**.
Use purple.

(hold) (most) (both) (both)

(don't) (both) (those) (both)

Read. Circle each **both**.

We got balls for

both of our cats.

We got yarn

for both of them, too.

Write **both** to complete each sentence.

Here are books for _____ girls.

I fed _____ of the fish.

Name: _____   Date: _____

Write **both**.

_____

- - - - - - - - - - - - - - - - - - -

_____

Connect the dots to spell **both**.
Find the word two times.

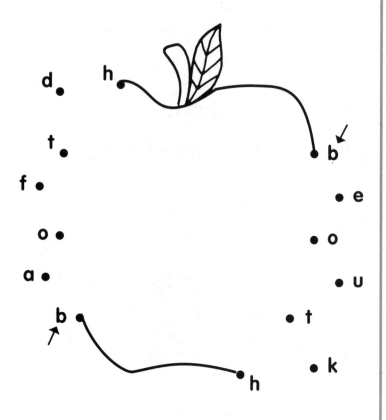

Write the missing letters
to spell **both**.

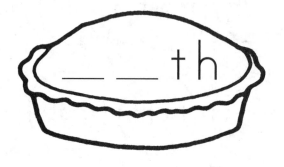

Color the glasses that have **both** on both sides. Use green.

Name: _____   Date: _____

sit

Trace **sit** two times. Use red, then blue.

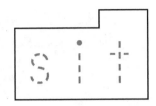

Help the kids get to the bus.
Color each space that has **sit**.
Use red.

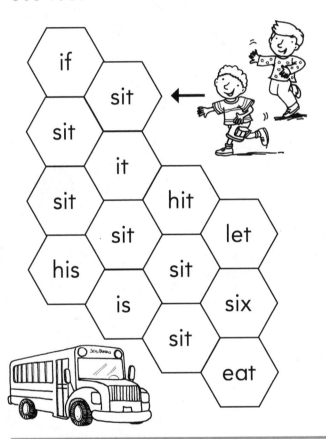

Read. Circle each **sit**.

I sit on the bus.

You sit on the bus.

We all sit on the bus

as it rides around the town.

Write **sit** to complete each sentence.

Go _____ at the desk.

Let's _____ in the back seat.

Name: _____ Date: _____

sit

Write **sit**.

_____

- - - - - - - - - - - - - - - - -

_____

Circle each **sit**.
Find the word five times.

c	s	i	t
g	i	f	j
e	t	h	s
s	i	t	i
i	f	c	t
t	j	u	g

Write the missing letters
to spell **sit**.

__ i __

S __ __

__ __ t

Help the car get to the Finish line. Trace the path that has **sit**.

sat — sat — sat — sit — sit — FINISH

sit — sit — sit — sat — sat

The Jumbo Book of Sight Word Practice Pages © 2013 by Immacula A. Rhodes, Scholastic Teaching Resources • page 368

Name: _____ Date: _____

which

Trace **which** two times. Use red, then blue.

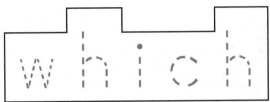

Color each butterfly that has **which**. Use blue.

which
what
wish
which
write
which
which
think

Read. Circle each **which**.

Tell which butterfly

you like best.

Tell which one

you choose.

Tell which color

is on its wings.

Is it yellow,

orange, or blue?

Write **which** to complete each sentence.

I know _____ bag is mine.

Did you see _____ way she went?

Name: _____   Date: _____

which

Write **which**.

_____

- - - - - - - - - - - - - - - - - -

_____

Find each spaceship that has **which**. Trace the path from that spaceship to the alien.

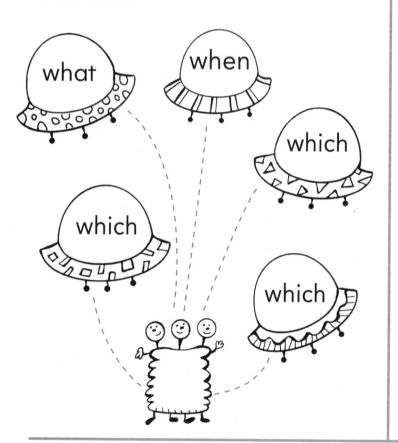

what

when

which

which

which

Write the missing letters to spell **which**.

_ h _ _ h

wh_ _ _ _

_ _ _ i _ _

Color each pair of cupcakes with the letters that spell **which**. Use blue.

wh   ich

wh   en

wh   at

wh   ich

Name: _____ Date: _____

Trace **read** two times. Use red, then blue.

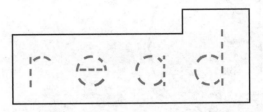

Color each book that has **read**.
Use yellow.

red

read

dear

read

read

real

rear

read

Read. Circle each **read**.

I read about people.

I read about pets.

I read just about

any book I can get!

Write **read** to complete each sentence.

This is the best book to _____.

I want to _____ her paper.

Name: _____ Date: _____

Write **read**.

_____

_ _

_____

Circle each **read**.
Find the word five times.

m r e a d h
k o d r x u
g n r e a d
i v h a c r
r e a d k e
v m o b u a
c n x i g d

Write the missing letters
to spell **read**.

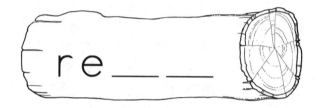

r e _ _ _ _

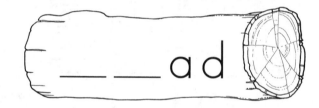

_ _ _ a d

r _ _ _ d

Color each turtle that has **read**. Use brown.

ride

read

read

dear

Name: _____ Date: _____

why

Trace **why** two times. Use red, then blue.

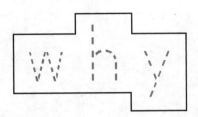

Color each bee that has **why**. Use yellow.

Read. Circle each **why**.

Please tell me why

the bees are flying.

Please tell me why

the bears are there.

If you know,

please tell me why.

Write **why** to complete each sentence.

Do you know _____ birds sing?

I don't know _____ I'm so tired.

Name: _____   Date: _____

why

Write **why**.

_____

_ _ _ _ _ _ _ _ _ _ _ _ _ _ _ _ _ _

_____

Find each acorn that has **why**. Trace the path from that acorn to the squirrel.

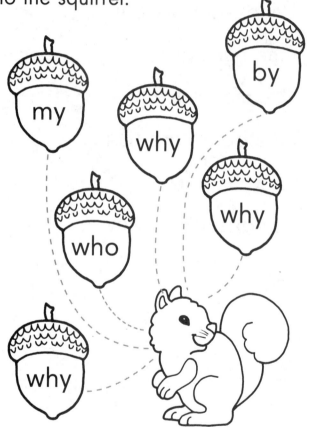

Write the missing letters to spell **why**.

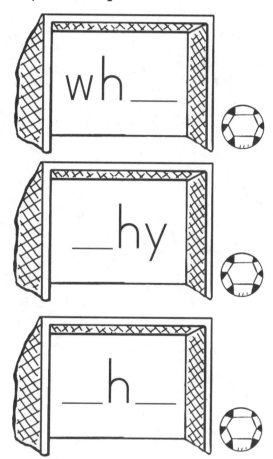

wh___

___hy

___h___

Color the two shoes with the letters that spell **why**. Use red.

Name: _____ Date: _____

Trace **found** two times. Use red, then blue.

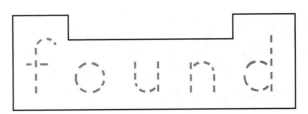

Color each bone that has **found**. Use brown.

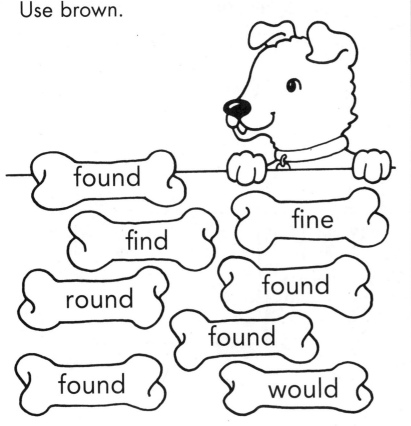

found

find

round

fine

found

found

found

would

Read. Circle each **found**.

My little dog
found one bone.
Then he found
many more, too.
Now he has found
all of the bones.
What do you
think he will do?

Write **found** to complete each sentence.

We _____ the teddy bear.

Our teacher _____ the ring.

Name: _____ Date: _____

Write **found**.

_____

- - - - - - - - - - - - - - - -

_____

Circle each **found**.
Find the word five times.

f o u n d s
o h e v a f
u g b i f o
n l t c o u
d s e h u n
i f o u n d
s b v g d e

Write the missing letters
to spell **found**.

__ o u n __

f __ __ __ n d

f o __ __ __ __

Color each robot that has **found**. Use purple.

round

found

found

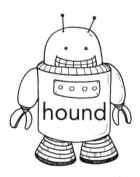
hound

Name: _____   Date: _____

because

Trace **because** two times. Use red, then blue.

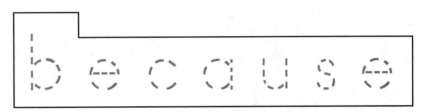

Color each lily pad that has **because**. Use green.

Read. Circle each **because**.

The frog ate a fly
because he was hungry.
Then he sat on a rock
because he was tired.

Write **because** to complete each sentence.

She cries _____ she is sad.

He hides _____ it's fun.

Name: _____   Date: _____

because

Write **because**.

_____

- - - - - - - - - - - - - - - - - -

_____

Help the chick get to the hen.
Trace the path with **because**.

Color each balloon that has
because. Draw a string from
that balloon to the fence.

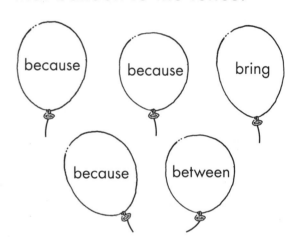

Write the missing letters
to spell **because**.

b __ c __ __ s __

__ e __ a u __ e

Name: _____ Date: _____

Trace **best** two times. Use red, then blue.

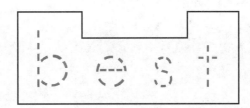

Help the kid get to the school.
Color each space that has **best**.
Use green.

Read. Circle each **best**.

I have the best teacher.

I'm in the best class.

I do my best at school.

I know I will pass!

Write **best** to complete each sentence.

The man wore his _____ vest.

We saw the _____ show today.

Name: _____   Date: _____

Write **best**.

_____

- - - - - - - - - - - - - - - - - - -

_____

Circle each **best**.
Find the word five times.

d	a	f	l	b	u
b	e	s	t	e	b
e	c	d	a	s	e
s	b	e	s	t	s
t	u	g	f	c	t

Write the missing letters
to spell **best**.

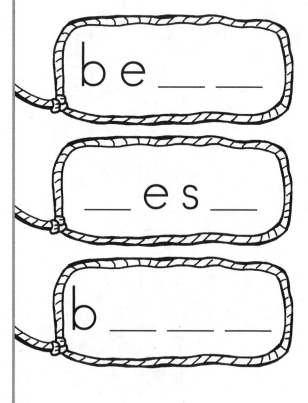

be ___ ___

___ e s ___

b ___ ___ ___

Color each pair of cows with the letters that spell **best**. Use red.

be st   be st   do es   be en

Name: _____ Date: _____

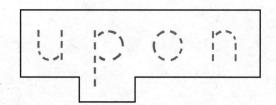

Trace **upon** two times. Use red, then blue.

Color each space that has **upon**. Use yellow.

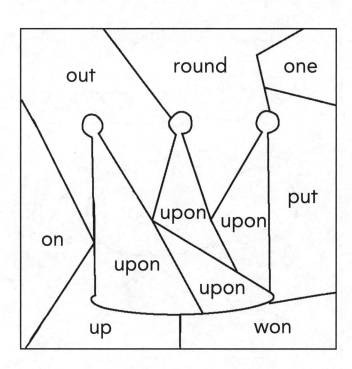

Read. Circle each **upon**.

The queen wore a crown

upon her head.

Then the queen sat

upon a throne.

Write **upon** to complete each sentence.

We came _____ a beehive.

Sit  _____ this horse.

Name: _____ Date: _____

Write **upon**.

_____

_____

_____

Help each raindrop get to the ground. Connect the dots to spell **upon**. Start at **u**.

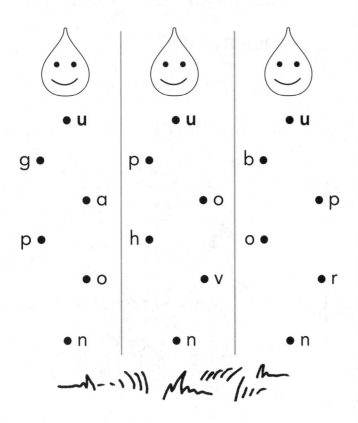

Write the missing letters to spell **upon**.

up ____ ____

____ ____ o n

____ p ____ n

Color each bat with the letters that spell **upon**. Use brown.

Name: _____ Date: _____

these

Trace **these** two times. Use red, then blue.

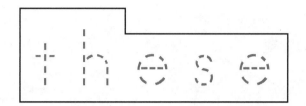

Color each grape that has **these**. Use purple.

Read. Circle each **these**.

I picked these grapes off of the vine.
Ant wants these grapes, but these grapes are all mine!

Write **these** to complete each sentence.

I need to wash _____ socks.

Use _____ bricks in the wall.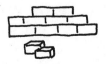

Name: _____ Date: _____

Write **these**.

_____

_____

_____

Circle each **these**.
Find the word five times.

t h e s e f b

a r t h e s e

t v l o g t w

h u f b x h o

e t h e s e r

s d o w u s a

e l g v f e d

Help the spider get to the web.
Trace the path with **these**.

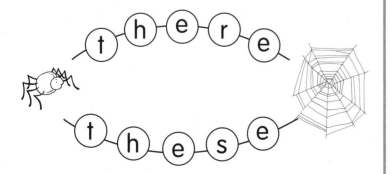

Color each ice-cream scoop
that has **these**. Draw a line
from that scoop to a cone.

Write the missing letters
to spell **these**.

t h __ __ __

__ __ __ e __ e

Name: _____ Date: _____

Trace **sing** two times. Use red, then blue.

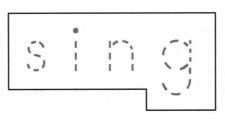

Color each mushroom that has **sing**. Use pink.

Read. Circle each **sing**.

Did you hear the fairy sing?

I heard her sing, too.

I liked the song

that she sang.

Let me sing it to you.

Write **sing** to complete each sentence.

Hear the bird _____.

I _____ with a band.

Name: _____   Date: _____

Write **sing**.

_____

- -

_____

Find each boat that has **sing**. Trace the path from that boat to the dock.

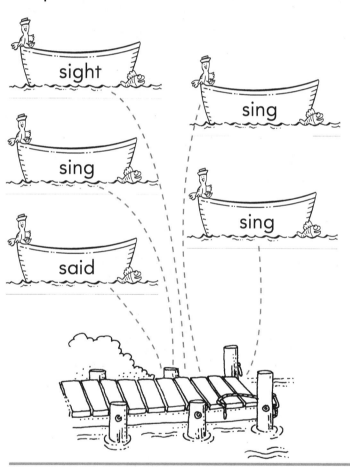

sight

sing

sing

said

sing

sing

Write the missing letters to spell **sing**.

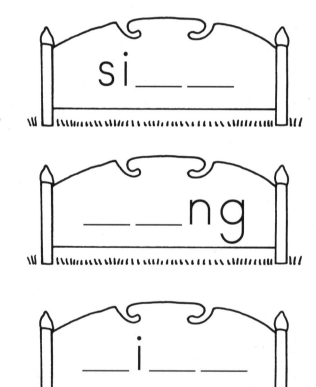

si _____

_____ ng

_____ i _____

Color each flower with the letters that spell **sing**. Use orange.

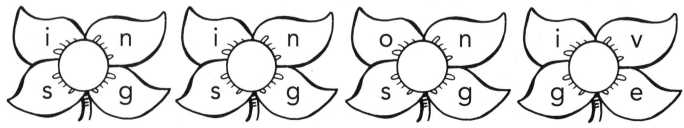

i n s g

i n s g

o n s g

i v g e

Name: _____   Date: _____

Trace **wish** two times. Use red, then blue.

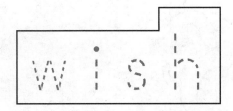

Color each candle that has **wish**. Use blue.

| will | wish | wish | want |

| wish | this | wish | with |

Read. Circle each **wish**.

Make a wish and

blow out the candles.

My wish is that

your wish comes true.

Write **wish** to complete each sentence.

We _____ the sun would come out.

I _____ I had a dog.

Name: _____ Date: _____

wish

Write **wish**.

_____

- - - - - - - - - - - - - - - - - - -

_____

Circle each **wish**.
Find the word five times.

w i s h w b
o w d u i n
w i s h s o
b s a v h d
u h w i s h

Write the missing letters
to spell **wish**.

W __ __ h

W i __ __

__ i s __

Color each fish bowl that has **wish**. Use blue.

 wish
 went
 wish
 will
 wish

Name: _____   Date: _____

many

Trace **many** two times. Use red, then blue.

many

Color each space that has **many**.
Use green.

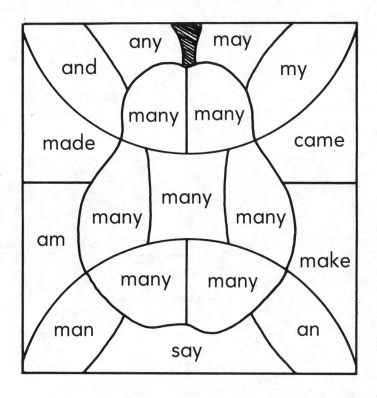

any   may
and   my
    many   many
made   came
        many
    many   many
am   make
    many   many
man   an
        say

Read. Circle each **many**.

I had many pears.

Yes, I had so many.

So I gave them all away.

Now I don't have any.

Write **many** to complete each sentence.

How _____ cups do you have?

I have so _____ flowers!

Name: _____ Date: _____

many

Write **many**.

_____

- - - - - - - - - - - - - - - -

_____

Find each ball that has **many**. Trace the path from that ball to the basket.

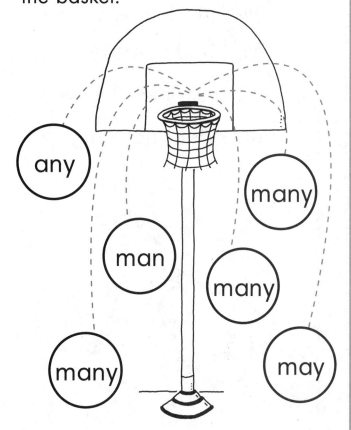

Write the missing letters to spell **many**.

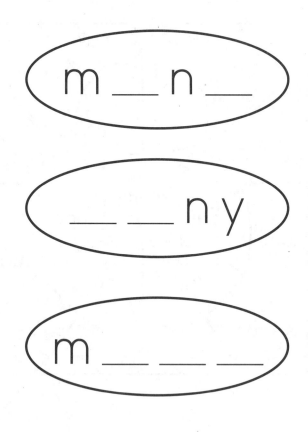

m __ n __

__ __ n y

m __ __ __ __

Color the two puzzle pieces with the letters that spell **many**. Use blue.

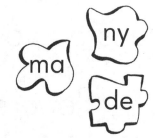

Name: _____   Date: _____

 **if**

Trace **if** two times. Use red, then blue.

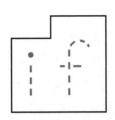

Help the girl get to the house.
Color each space that has **if**.
Use brown.

it   in   to

if   if   if

of   if   is

off   if   on

if

if   at

Read. Circle each **if**.

Come in if it is raining.

Stay out if the sun

is shining.

Write **if** to complete each sentence.

Get some milk _____ you want some.

Go to bed _____ you are sleepy.

Name: _____   Date: _____

Write **if** two times.

_____   _____

_____   _____

Find each hippo that has **if**.
Trace its path to the water.

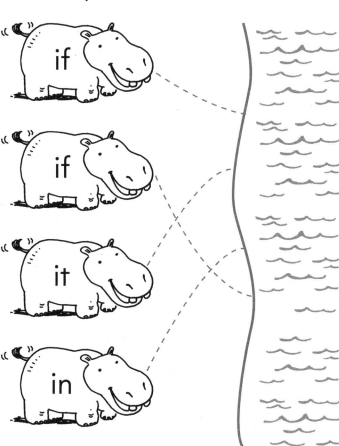

Write **if** on each tent.

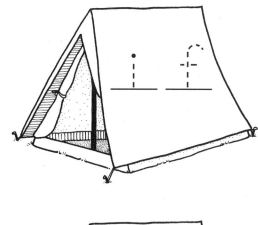

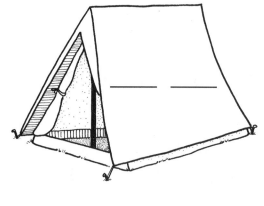

Color each pair of flowers with the letters that spell **if**. Use purple.

Name: _____ Date: _____

Trace **long** two times. Use red, then blue.

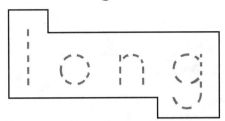

Color each space that has **long**. Use green.

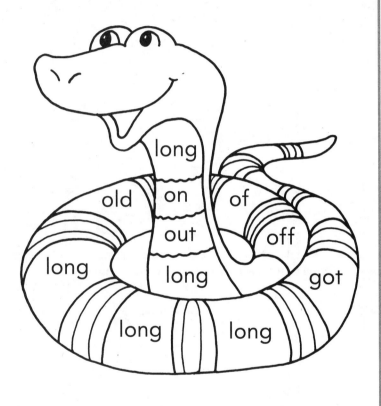

Read. Circle each **long**.

I saw a long snake

on a long and hot day.

He went into a long log,

then he slithered away.

Write **long** to complete each sentence.

This is a _____ rope.

The giraffe has a _____ neck.

Name: _____   Date: _____

Write **long**.

_____

_____

Connect the dots to spell **long**.
Find the word two times.

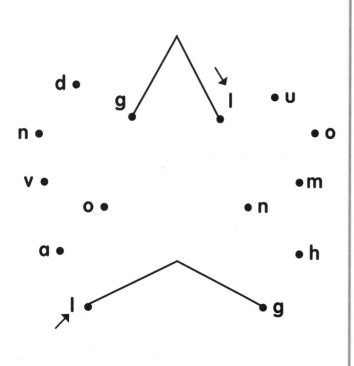

Write the missing letters to spell **long**.

l ___ ___ g

___ ___ n g

l o ___ ___

Color each yo-yo that has **long**. Use red.

lost

long

long

long

loud

Name: _____ Date: _____

 about

Trace **about** two times. Use red, then blue.

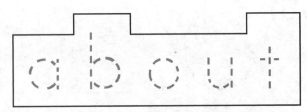

Help the kid get to the book.
Color each space that has **about**.
Use orange.

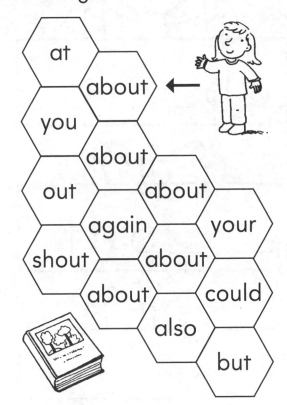

Read. Circle each **about**.

You can read about

places to go.

You can read about

how to cook.

You can read about

most anything.

You can read about

it in a book.

Write **about** to complete each sentence.

The time is _____ noon.

She wrote _____ dogs.

Name: _____ Date: _____

about

Write **about**.

_____

- - - - - - - - - - - - - - - - - - - -

_____

Circle each **about**.
Find the word five times.

g a b o u t
a b o u t a
k o n f e b
f u l v d o
n t w g h u
a b o u t t

Write the missing letters
to spell **about**.

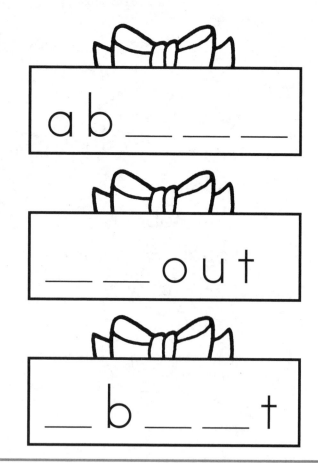

a b _ _ _ _

_ _ _ o u t

_ b _ _ t

Color each pair of cupcakes with the letters that spell **about**. Use red.

Name: _____ Date: _____

Trace **got** two times. Use red, then blue.

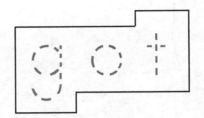

Color each space that has **got**.
Use green.

Read. Circle each **got**.

We got a pet fish.

We got a pet bird.

We got a pet turtle—

it's the best pet yet!

Write **got** to complete each sentence.

The sky _____ very cloudy.

We _____ chips to eat.

Name: _____   Date: _____

Write **got**.

_____

- - - - - - - - - - - - - - - - - - -

_____

Help each bowling ball get to its pin. Connect the dots to spell **got**. Start at **g**.

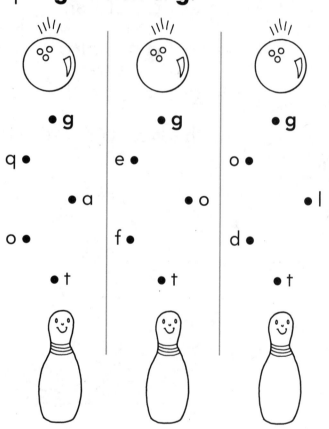

Write the missing letters to spell **got**.

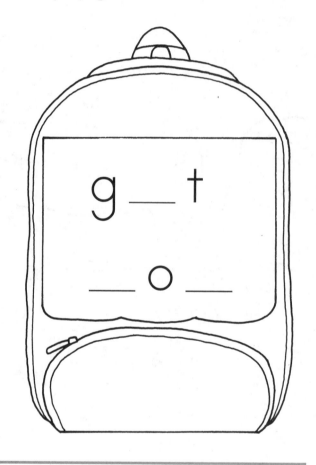

g _ t

_ o _

Color each set of candles with the letters that spell **got**. Use orange.

g o t

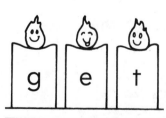

g e t

a t e

g o t

Name: _____ Date: _____

six

Trace **six** two times. Use red, then blue.

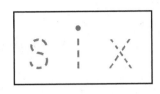

Color each space that has **six**.
Use orange.

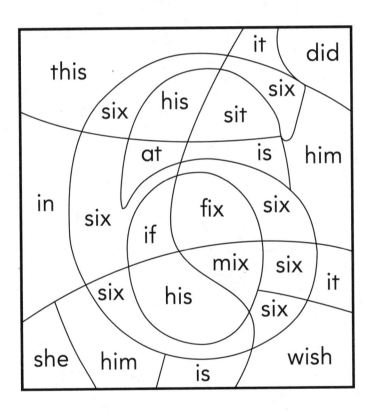

Read. Circle each **six**.

I have six crayons.

No color is the same.

I used my six crayons

to write my name.

Write **six** to complete each sentence.

The _____ birds ate their seeds.

A plane went by _____ times.

six

Write **six**.

_____

- - - - - - - - - - - - -

_____

Find each fish that has **six**.
Trace its path to the water.

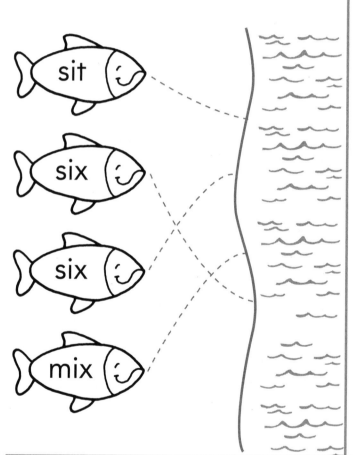

sit

six

six

mix

Write the missing letters
to spell **six**.

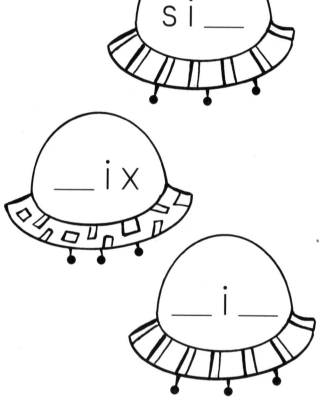

s i __

__ i x

__ i __

Color each part of the caterpillar that has **six**. Use red.

six sit it six six is if six six his

Name: _____ Date: _____

never

Trace **never** two times. Use red, then blue.

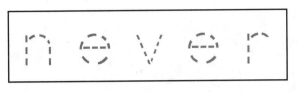

Help the rocket get to the moon. Color each cloud that has **never**. Use gray.

Read. Circle each **never**.

I've never been in a rocket.

I've never walked on the moon.

I've never gone through space,

but I hope to do that soon!

Write **never** to complete each sentence.

I _____ touch a hot grill.

We _____ use our fan.

Name: _____ Date: _____

Write **never**.

_____

- - - - - - - - - - - - - - - - - - -

_____

Draw a line from each frog to the lily pad that has **never**.

never

over

never

every

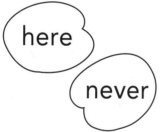

here

never

Write the missing letters to spell **never**.

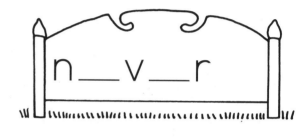

n__v__r

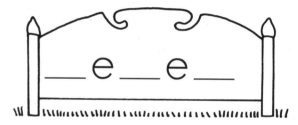

__e__e__

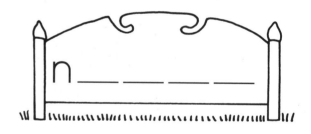

n_____

Color each chick that has **never**. Use yellow.

every   never   never   ever   never

Name: _____   Date: _____

seven

Trace **seven** two times. Use red, then blue.

Color each space that has **seven**.
Use red.

Read. Circle each **seven**.

There once was a rooster
with seven feathers in his tail.
He got up seven days a week
and began to yell,
"Cock-a-doodle-doo!
Good morning to you!"

Write **seven** to complete each sentence.

Her wedding is at _____.

There are _____ days in a week.

Name: _____ Date: _____

seven

Write **seven**.

_____

- - - - - - - - - - - - - - - - - - -

_____

Find each seal that has **seven**.
Trace its path to the rocks.

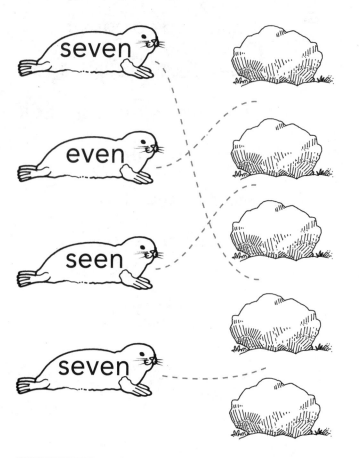

Write the missing letters
to spell **seven**.

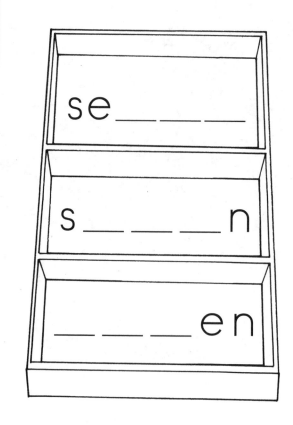

se _ _ _ _

s _ _ _ _ n

_ _ _ _ e n

Color the boxes with the letters that spell **seven**. Use orange.

a	o	x	r	m
s	c	v	e	h
g	e	w	z	n

s	r	w	a	n
x	e	z	e	m
o	c	v	y	h

Name: _____   Date: _____

Trace **eight** two times. Use red, then blue.

Color each egg that has **eight**. Use yellow.

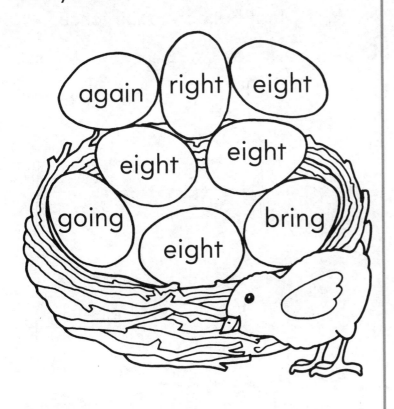

again right eight
eight eight
going bring
eight

Read. Circle each **eight**.

Hen laid eight eggs

in a nest.

The eight eggs

each held a chick.

When the eight eggs hatch,

take any chick you pick.

Write **eight** to complete each sentence.

We will plant _____ seeds.

The train ride is _____ hours.

Name: _____   Date: _____

eight

Write **eight**.

_____

- - - - - - - - - - - - - - - - - - - -

_____

Circle each **eight**.
Find the word five times.

r e i g h t q
v o m f e k u
y n r e i l m
x q e i g h t
k o l g h a v
e i g h t m y
l f u t c n w

Color each balloon that has
eight. Draw a string from
that balloon to the fence.

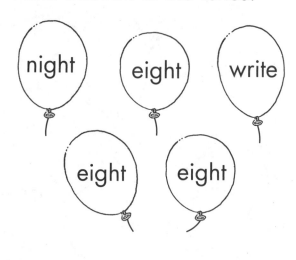

night   eight   write

eight   eight

eight

Help the chick get to the hen.
Trace the path with **eight**.

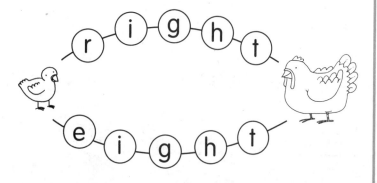

r i g h t

e i g h t

Write the missing letters
to spell **eight**.

e i ___ ___ t

___ ___ g h ___

Name: _____ Date: _____

 today

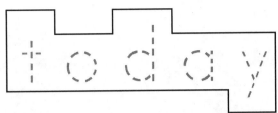
Trace **today** two times. Use red, then blue.

today

Color each space that has **today**.
Use purple.

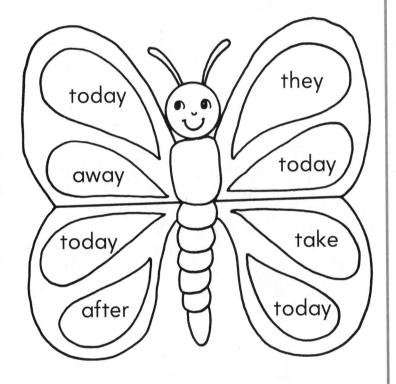

today   they

away   today

today   take

after   today

Read. Circle each **today**.

A butterfly came by today.

A ladybug came by today, too.

And when the two

came by today,

I sent them to see you!

Write **today** to complete each sentence.

We are going to the zoo _____!

I ate an apple _____ at lunch.

Name: _____   Date: _____

today

Write **today**.

_____

_____

_____

Circle each **today**.
Find the word five times.

t o d a y c t
o h u b f e o
d t o d a y d
a c x h e b a
y w t o d a y

Write the missing letters
to spell **today**.

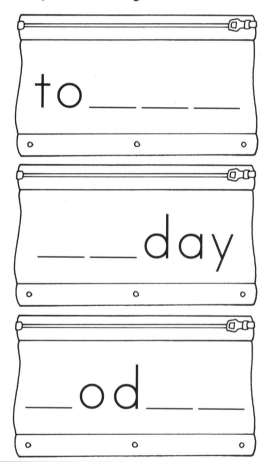

to_____

___day

_od_____

Color each pair of pears with the letters that spell **today**. Use yellow.

th ose   to day   ta ken   to day

Name: _____   Date: _____

myself

Trace **myself** two times. Use red, then blue.

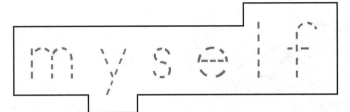
myself

Color each space that has **myself**.
Use brown.

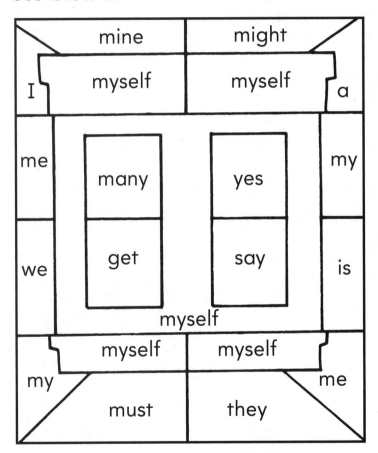

mine	might
myself	myself
many	yes
get	say
myself
myself	myself
must	they

I · me · we · my · a · my · is · me

Read. Circle each **myself**.

I see myself in a mirror

when I look in it as I pass.

Sometimes, when I look

in a window,

I see myself in the glass.

Write **myself** to complete each sentence.

I made _____ a drink.

I sent the letters _____.

Name: _____   Date: _____

myself

Write **myself**.

_____

- - - - - - - - - - - - - - - - - - - -

_____

Circle each **myself**.
Find the word five times.

a m y s e l f
m y s e l f m
c s u r n o y
w e k g x r s
x l j w a t e
g f n u k h l
t m y s e l f

Color each ice-cream scoop that has **myself**. Draw a line from that scoop to a cone.

Help the spider get to the web.
Trace the path with **myself**.

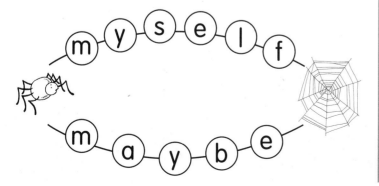

Write the missing letters to spell **myself**.

___ ___ self

my ___ ___ ___ ___

Name: _____   Date: _____

Trace **much** two times. Use red, then blue.

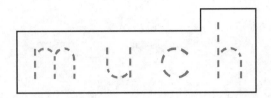

Color each space that has **much**.
Use purple.

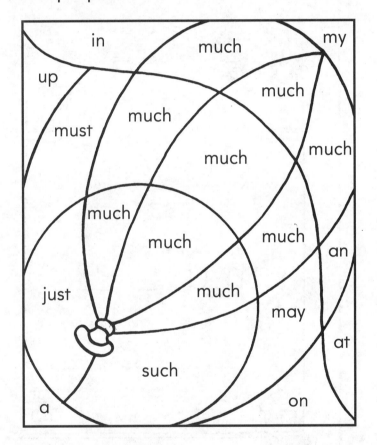

Read. Circle each **much**.

I blew too much air
before I stopped.
My balloon got too tight,
and so it popped!

Write **much** to complete each sentence.

I ate too _____ pie.

How _____ does the tie cost?

Name: _____ Date: _____

much

Write **much**.

_____

- - - - - - - - - - - - - - - - - - - -

_____

Help each crow get to the corn.
Connect the dots to spell **much**.
Start at **m**.

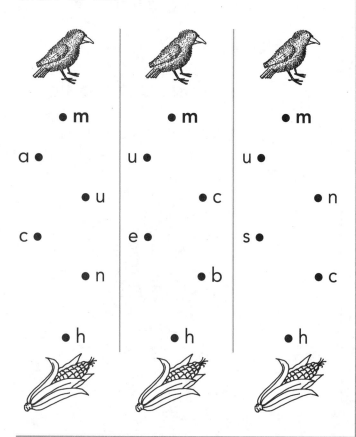

•m   •m   •m

a•   u•   u•

    •u   •c   •n

c•   e•   s•

    •n   •b   •c

•h   •h   •h

Write the missing letters
to spell **much**.

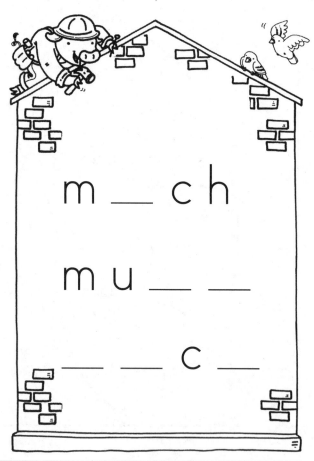

m __ c h

m u __ __

__ __ c __

Color each pair of cookies with the letters that spell **much**. Use yellow.

mu   ch

mu   ch

mu   st

Name: _____   Date: _____

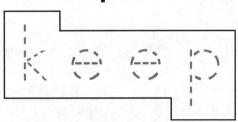

keep

Trace **keep** two times. Use red, then blue.

Help the kid get to the frog. Color each grass patch that has **keep**. Use green.

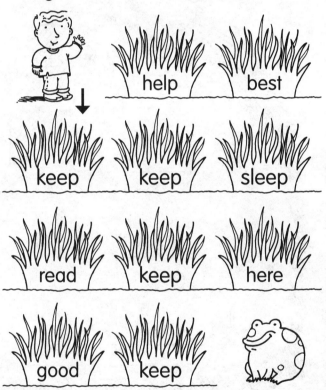

help	best
keep	keep	sleep
read	keep	here
good	keep

Read. Circle each **keep**.

Can I keep this lizard?

Can I keep this snake?

Can I keep this frog?

What good pets

they all will make!

Write **keep** to complete each sentence.

You can _____ this book.

I _____ my room clean.

Name: _____ Date: _____

keep

Write **keep**.

_____

_____

_____

Find each spider that has **keep**.
Trace its path to the spout.

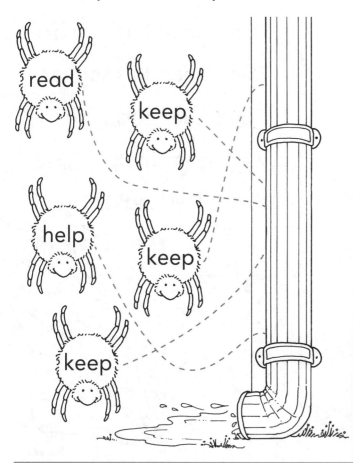

read

keep

help

keep

keep

Write the missing letters
to spell **keep**.

k _ _ p

_ e e _

k _ _ _ _

Circle each **keep**.
Find the word five times.

k e e p c k

e h b a d e

e k e e p e

p a k e e p

Name: _____ Date: _____

Trace **try** two times. Use red, then blue.

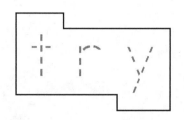

Color each float that has **try**.
Use yellow.

Read. Circle each **try**.

I will try to swim.

I will try to dive.

I will try.

I will try.

I will try and try!

Write **try** to complete each sentence.

Will you _____ on this shirt?

He will _____ to fly the kite.

Name: _____ Date: _____

Write **try**.

_____

- - - - - - - - - - - - - - - - - - - -

_____

Circle each **try**.
Find the word five times.

t	r	y	a
r	h	i	k
y	l	x	t
n	f	u	r
i	t	r	y
t	r	y	w

Write the missing letters
to spell **try**.

t r __

__ r __

__ __ y

Color the set of friends with the letters that spell **try**. Use orange.

Name: _____   Date: _____

start

Trace **start** two times. Use red, then blue.

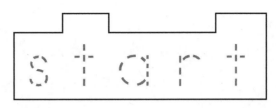

Color each flower that has **start**.
Use pink.

stand start first start

fast start start thank

Read. Circle each **start**.

It's the start of spring—

this is how I know:

Days start to warm up,

and flowers start to grow.

Write **start** to complete each sentence.

It's time for school to _____.

Did the rain _____ just now?

Name: _____   Date: _____

Write **start**.

_____

- - - - - - - - - - - - - - - - - - - -

_____

Circle each **start**.
Find the word five times.

c	o	s	t	a	r	t
l	h	t	i	n	d	u
s	t	a	r	t	o	s
e	d	r	u	g	b	t
b	n	t	c	f	l	a
i	s	t	a	r	t	r
g	f	o	c	h	e	t

Color each kite that has **start**. Draw a string from that kite to the kangaroo.

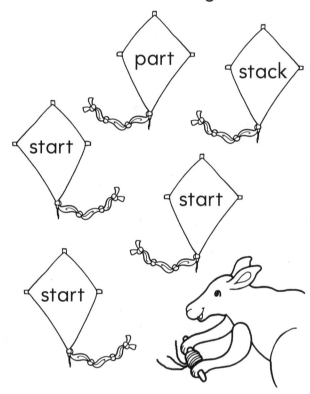

part

stack

start

start

start

Help the lizard get to the rock.
Trace the path with **start**.

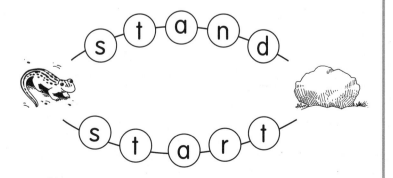

s t a n d

s t a r t

Write the missing letters to spell **start**.

s t __ __ t

s __ __ r __

Name: _____   Date: _____

 ten

Trace **ten** two times. Use red, then blue.

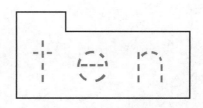

Color each star that has **ten**.
Use yellow.

Read. Circle each **ten**.

There were ten stars

in the sky last night.

Those ten little stars

made ten little nights.

Write **ten** to complete each sentence.

You hide while I count to _____.

I have a ball and _____ jacks.

Name: _____   Date: _____

ten

Write **ten**.

_____

_____

Find each rabbit that has **ten**.
Trace its path to the woods.

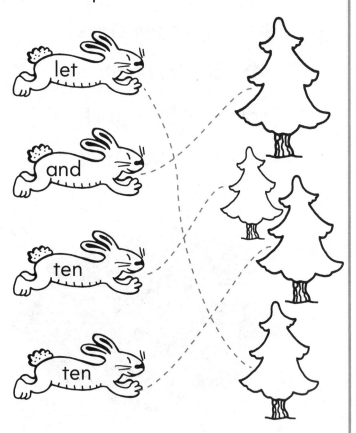

Write the missing letters
to spell **ten**.

t __ __

__ e __

Color each banner that has **ten**. Use blue.

| ten | ten | her | ten | the | ten | tan | ten | ten |

Name: _____ Date: _____

bring

Trace **bring** two times. Use red, then blue.

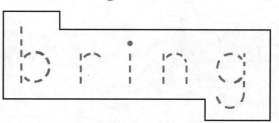

Help the kid get to the pizza. Color each space that has **bring**. Use red.

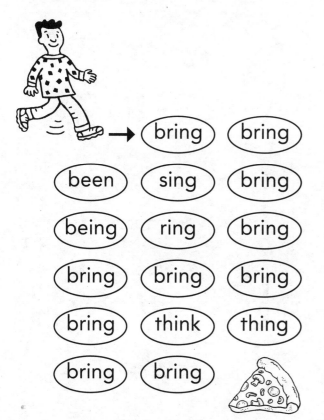

bring	bring
been	sing	bring
being	ring	bring
bring	bring	bring
bring	think	thing
bring	bring	

Read. Circle each **bring**.

Will you bring pizza

for all of us to eat?

And also bring cookies

for a nice, sweet treat!

Write **bring** to complete each sentence.

Let me _____ you some cake.

I will _____ my lunch today.

Name: _____ Date: _____

 bring

Write **bring**.

_____

_____

_____

Help each giraffe get to its tree.
Trace the path with **bring**.

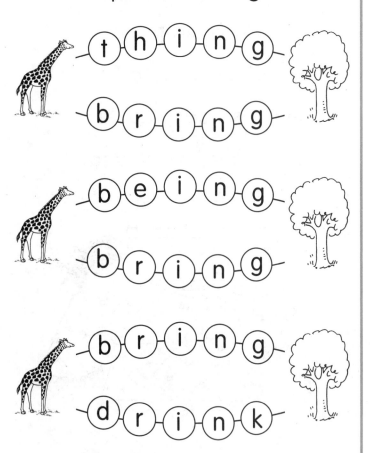

Write the missing letters
to spell **bring**.

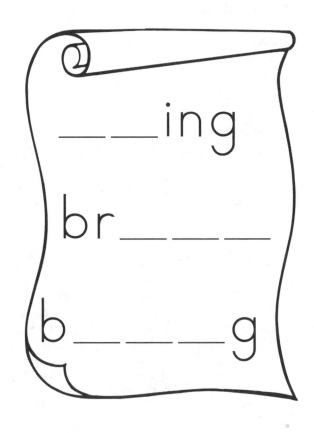

___ ing

br _____

b _____ g

Color each turtle that has **bring**. Use green.

think

bring

bring

doing

Name: _____ Date: _____

Trace **drink** two times. Use red, then blue.

Color each cup that has **drink**.
Use purple.

bring

drink

drink

think

right

drink

drink

ring

Read. Circle each **drink**.

Take a cup.

Take a drink.

What is the drink?

What do you think?

Write **drink** to complete each sentence.

I want a _____ of milk.

Dad likes ice in his _____.

Name: _____   Date: _____

Write **drink**.

_____

- - - - - - - - - - - - - - - - - -

_____

Draw a line from each frog to the lily pad that has **drink**.

bring
drink

drink
think

thing
drink

Write the missing letters to spell **drink**.

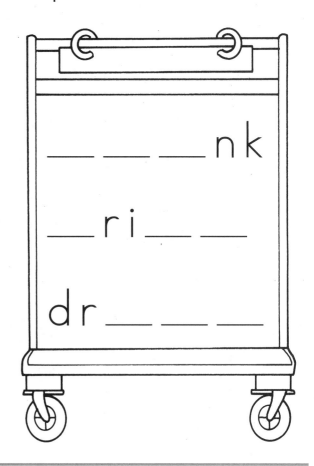

_ _ _ _ n k

_ r i _ _ _

d r _ _ _ _

Color the boxes with the letters that spell **drink**. Use orange.

d	r	l	m	f
p	x	i	n	t
b	u	j	w	k

q	x	y	u	k
d	b	i	n	h
p	r	l	m	f

Name: _____   Date: _____

Trace **only** two times. Use red, then blue.

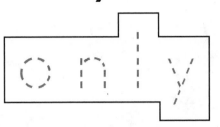

Color each space that has **only**.
Use red.

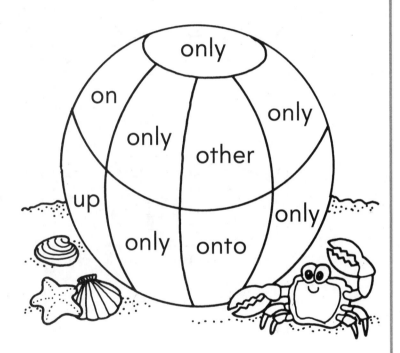

Read. Circle each **only**.

I have only one ball.

My only ball is round.

My ball is the only one

sitting on the ground.

Write **only** to complete each sentence.

There is _____ one fish.

These are my _____ shoes.

Name: _____   Date: _____

Write **only**.

_____

_____

_____

Help each sheep get to its barn.
Trace the path with **only**.

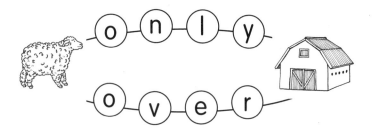

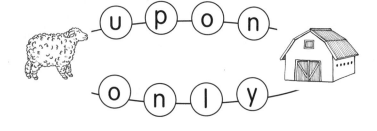

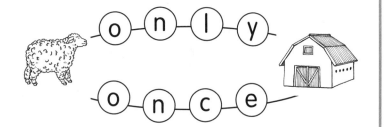

Write the missing letters
to spell **only**.

on_____

_nl__

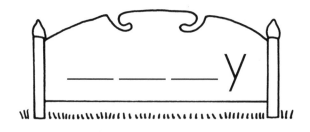

_____y

Color each bird that has **only**. Use blue.

open   only   onto   only

The Jumbo Book of Sight Word Practice Pages © 2013 by Immacula A. Rhodes, Scholastic Teaching Resources • page 426

Name: _____   Date: _____

Trace **better** two times. Use red, then blue.

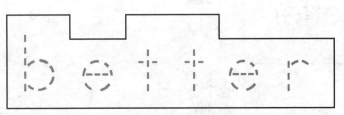

Color each space that has **better**.
Use purple.

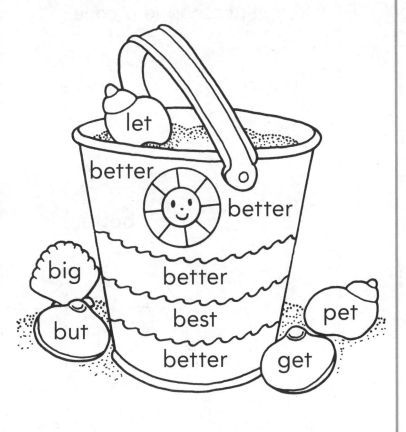

Read. Circle each **better**.

Is it better to find shells

or to play in the sand?

Which do you like better?

Tell me, if you can.

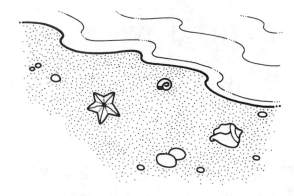

Write **better** to complete each sentence.

We'd _____ wait for the bus.

I like a dog _____ than a cat.

Name: _____ Date: _____

better

Write **better**.

_____

- - - - - - - - - - - - - - - -

_____

Circle each **better**.
Find the word five times.

b e t t e r a
e u d o v b f
t b e t t e r
t o w u l t m
e f n f u t k
r m a w v e l
b e t t e r n

Help the spider get to the web.
Trace the path with **better**.

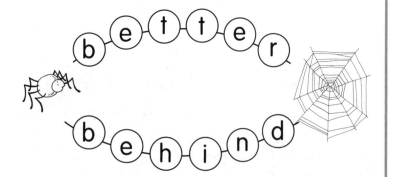

Color each ice-cream scoop
that has **better**. Draw a line
from that scoop to a cone.

Write the missing letters
to spell **better**.

b __ t __ __ r

__ e __ __ e __

The Jumbo Book of Sight Word Practice Pages © 2013 by Immacula A. Rhodes, Scholastic Teaching Resources • page 428

Name: _____ Date: _____

Trace **hold** two times. Use red, then blue.

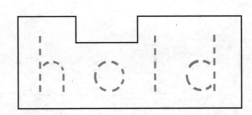

Color each space that has **hold**.
Use yellow.

| hold | would | hold | help |
| who | hold | held | hold |

Read. Circle each **hold**.

This basket can hold
your apple.
This basket can hold
your pear.
You can even use
this basket to hold
your teddy bear.

Write **hold** to complete each sentence.

You can _____ my rabbit.

This cage will _____ the birds.

Name: _____ Date: _____

Write **hold**.

_____

- - - - - - - - - - - - - - - - -

_____

Find each **hold**.
Find the word five times.

t h u i b h
h o l d h o
i l a t o l
e d h o l d
b u k f d e

Write the missing letters
to spell **hold**.

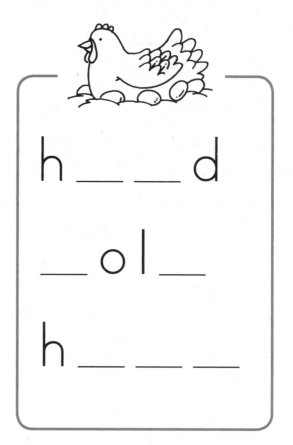

h _ _ d

_ o l _

h _ _ _ _

Color each clover with the letters that spell **hold**. Use green.

Name: _____ Date: _____

Trace **warm** two times. Use red, then blue.

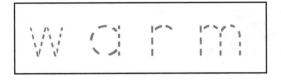

Help the lizard get to the rock. Color each grass patch that has **warm**. Use green.

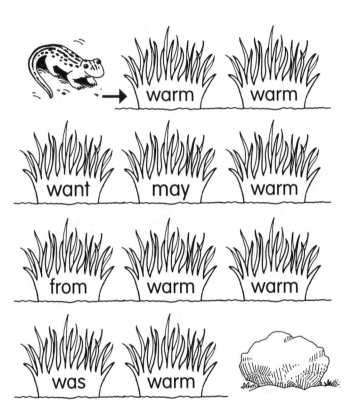

Read. Circle each **warm**.

Lizard wanted to get warm.

A rock was in the warm sun.

Lizard got on the rock.

And there, Lizard got warm.

Write **warm** to complete each sentence.

Do you want a _____ drink?

Put on a coat to stay _____.

Name: _____   Date: _____

Write **warm**.

_____

_____

_____

Draw a line from each snake to the log that has **warm**.

   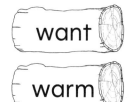

want

warm

was

warm

    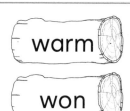

warm

won

Write the missing letters to spell **warm**.

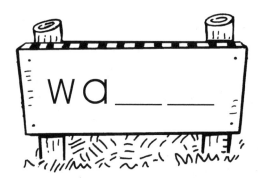

W a _____

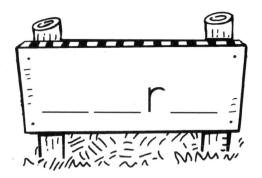

_____ r _____

Color each pig that has **warm**. Use pink.

down   warm   warm   some